W9-ANR-470

"Rabbi Korngold serves as a spiritual guide through the myriad paths in the great outdoors where one can re-create the conditions conducive to experiencing God. A wonderfully written book for Jews and non-Jews alike." —*Richard D. Bank, author of* The Everything Judaism Book

"*God in the Wilderness* is an intelligent and insightful book that helps us think outside of the box about religion, God, and our place in the Universe." —*Frederic Luskin, Ph.D., director of the Stanford University Forgiveness Project, and author of* Forgive for Good

"Rabbi Jamie knows that nature's sensuousness, lucidity, and God are fundamental to human health, if not one and the same."

—*John Fielder, photographer*

"I felt like I had found a hidden treasure in *God in the Wilderness* as I became more enveloped by its omnipotent wisdom."

—*Randine Lewis, L.Ac., Ph.D., author of* The Way of the Fertile Soul

"*God in the Wilderness* is not the religion of our fathers and our mothers. But it is the religion of our patriarchs and our matriarchs. And it may be the kind of religious experience our children and their children will celebrate." —*Rabbi Kenneth E. Ehrlich, dean, Hebrew Union College*

"I expected that *God in the Wilderness* would be honest, passionate, and spiritual. It is all these things. It is also earthy, funny, and downright practical." —*Murray Suid, author of* Words of a Feather

"Our spiritual sages first sensed God in the garden, in the desert, on the mountain. As civilization grew, God's voice was filtered through interpretation and law and institution. Rabbi Jamie Korngold takes us back into the wilderness, where we rediscover our humility and humanity and God." —*Elyse Frishman, editor,* Mishkan T'filah

"A tremendous read and inspiring story for anyone who wants to get closer to the earth." —*Adam Werbach, founder and CEO, Act Now*

"This book speaks to people of all faiths who have a hunger for reconnecting with the God of their own understandings and traditions."

—*Trudy Harris, R.N., author of* Glimpses of Heaven

# God in the Wilderness

Rediscovering the Spirituality
of the Great Outdoors
with the Adventure Rabbi

## Rabbi Jamie S. Korngold

**Doubleday**

New York   London   Toronto   Sydney   Auckland

PUBLISHED BY DOUBLEDAY

Published in the United States by Doubleday, an
imprint of The Doubleday Broadway Publishing
Group, a division of Random House, Inc., New
York. www.doubleday.com

DOUBLEDAY and the portrayal of an anchor with
a dolphin are registered trademarks of Random
House, Inc.

Biblical quotations are from the JPS Tanakh, unless
otherwise attributed to the Jerusalem Bible by
Koren (JB), Soncino Classics Collection (Soncino),
or the author's translation.

*Book design by Donna Sinisgalli*

Library of Congress Cataloging-in-Publication Data

Korngold, Jamie S.
    God in the wilderness : rediscovering the spir-
    ituality of the great outdoors with the adventure
    rabbi / Jamie S. Korngold.
        p. cm.
    1. Spiritual life—Judaism. 2. Nature—Reli-
    gious aspects—Judaism. 3. Hiking. 4. Bible.
    O.T.—Criticism, interpretation, etc. 5. Korn-
    gold, Jamie S.—Travel. I. Title.

    BM723.K68 2007
    296.7—dc22

                                    2007005340

ISBN 978-0-385-52049-2

PRINTED IN THE UNITED STATES OF AMERICA

10  9  8  7  6  5  4  3  2

To my parents,

*Bob and Carole Korngold,*

*who taught me to follow my dreams*

To my husband,

*Jeff Finkelstein,*

*who makes my dreams come true*

# Contents

CHAPTER 7

Restore Your Soul Beside Still Waters

AFTERWORD

Guardians of the Earth: To Till and to
Tend

# Acknowledgments

*Thank you to*

My talented literary agent, Carol Susan Roth of Author's Best, for calling one autumn morning and asking if I would write a book. She skillfully guided me through every step of the process from contemplation to completion.

The team at Doubleday Religion, including Bill Barry, Trace Murphy, Maggie Carr, and most of all my editor, Darya Porat, for their commitment to bringing this project to fruition.

Jon Stewart and *The Daily Show* for teaching me that if you phrase it as a question you can't be wrong.

Toby Ziegler of *The West Wing* (and therefore Richard Schiff and Aaron Sorkin) for teaching me that the antidote for Writer's Block is to eat more pie. (Costco's eight-pound All-American Chocolate Cake also works well.)

My husband, Jeff, and daughter, Sadie, for keeping me well supplied with chocolate cake.

Rhoda Lewin, whose ability to add a comma here and substitute a word there improved this text immeasurably.

Rabbi Mike Comins, Rabbi Dan Fink, Ellen Bernstein, Rabbi David E. Stein—my friends and guides—for scouting the trail.

My daughter Sadie's teachers, led by Martha S., for taking such precious care of her while I wrote.

The families of Adam Mathew Barron (the kayaker) and Dr. Nelson Gantz (the doctor); may their memories be for a blessing.

The thousands of participants on Adventure Rabbi programs who have shared their insights with me over many miles of trails.

The Adventure Rabbi Leadership Council for helping create this vision and working side by side with me to build our Adventure Rabbi community.

And most of all, thank you to my husband, Jeff Finkelstein, who helped with every idea and phrase in this text. Without his tenacity, without his passionate belief in me and what I do, these pages would surely be blank and I would be an indoor pulpit rabbi preaching sermons in synagogues rather than teaching on mountaintops.

# God in the Wilderness

# Genesis of the Adventure Rabbi

*In the beginning, God created the heaven and
the earth.*

—Genesis 1:1 (Soncino)

When the phone rang, I hesitated before answering. It was
a tightly scheduled afternoon. Was there time for a call?

"It's Bernice," said my assistant.

My eyes immediately turned to the painting on the
wall of the Colorado River snaking through the red and
purple rocks of the Grand Canyon. Bernice and her husband, Scott, had given me the painting as an ordination gift
when I became a rabbi. I hung it on the wall of my rabbinic
study to remind me that the roots of Judaism are the
desert, streams, and mountains—the wilderness where
our religion was created and where the Torah was received.

Would our ancestors even recognize the Judaism of today, filled with Sabbath and holiday services, prayer books and board meetings? The massive canyon walls urge me not to forget that for centuries before the People of the Book (the Jews) had a book (the Bible) or prayer books, synagogues or rabbis for that matter, they met with God in the wilderness, on mountains, and by streams. The e-mails overflowing my in-box suddenly seemed less pressing, and I picked up the phone.

"It's Bernice and Scott," said the excited voices on the other end of the line. Their news came tumbling out, as if each word was trying to jump in front of the next. After anxiously waiting for months, they had finally heard from their adoption agency. A baby girl was waiting for them in Romania. Scott was taking a short leave from Williams College, where he directed the Outdoor Program, and they were leaving that night to bring her home.

"She isn't Jewish," Bernice explained, "so we need to do a conversion ceremony along with the baby naming. We want to do it in the base of the Grand Canyon, since that has always been such a special place to us."

Scott chimed in, "It's our Holy of Holies. We can use the Colorado River as our mikvah. We'll bring a group of Williams students to be our congregation. Will you come? Will you officiate?"

It was January. I was living in Calgary, Canada, where winter is bleak and bitter cold, despite the occasional warm winds, or chinooks, which blow off the mountains. And the legendary skiing for which I had moved to Canada had failed to materialize. We were in a three-year drought. I looked out my window, already dark at three in the after-noon. "I'll be there," I said.

For many people, including Bernice and Scott, the Grand Canyon is a spiritual haven, taking us back to the days before asphalt and shopping malls dominated the land-scape. Geologists like to say that hiking into the Grand Canyon is like traveling back through history. What they mean is that the rocks at the base, the inner gorge of black schist, are over two billion years old, the oldest exposed rock in the world. Above this base lie sequential layers of younger rocks, because over millions of years, as ancient seas advanced and then retreated, and then advanced again, the sands of the seabed left behind layers of limestone, sandstone, and shale. These stunning layers, now red, yel-low, orange, and purple, make up the striking horizontal bands visible on the upper canyon walls. As the centuries passed, the rivers and tributary streams also carved through the rocks, creating the walls, plateaus, and promontories we now call the "temples" of the Grand Canyon—to some people, the Holy of Holies.

Even today, as you hike down the canyon you witness the ongoing weathering of the rock by the wind and the water seeping through the cracks, tenaciously peeling back the layers of time. With each switchback of the trail, you descend closer toward the very beginning of time, to the soul of the earth.

Those of us who love wilderness excursions know that when we are open to a spiritual experience, hiking also exposes the layers of the soul. Perhaps this is why God chose to give us the Torah in the wilderness, to ensure that we were spiritually prepared to hear the teachings. With each mile of distance from civilization, as packs seem to grow heavier and the footing more tenuous, we embark on an internal journey into the core of our selves.

What is it about nature that provides such a rich spiritual experience? Why historically was wilderness an integral part of Judaism?

Removed from the distractions of everyday life, of cell phones, e-mails, and to-do lists, we are able to immerse ourselves fully in the moment, in each step, in each breath. As we leave behind the safety of homes and cars, and we step fully into the wilderness to meet nature, we also meet ourselves. As we look outward to the wilderness, we look inward and reawaken to what is essential in our lives, to the core of our being.

Perhaps the sense of spirituality is created by the bond that forms between people in the wilderness. Undistracted by our daily routines, we give each other our full attention, truly hearing each other's words. We come to know the essence of each other's being. We depend on one another, quite literally trusting each other with our lives. There is a bond between those who have traveled the wilderness together that is unlike any other. Not surprisingly, it was in the wilderness that a ragtag group of slaves bonded together and became the People Israel.

Perhaps the heightened spirituality comes from the physical exertion that keeps us journeying inward, forcing us to savor each breath and appreciate each step. In the wild, we push ourselves beyond what we thought was physically possible and come to know our true physical and emotional capabilities.

But it is more than physical. Many of us have had this same spiritual uplift when we read the nature poetry of Walt Whitman or looked at Ansel Adams's photograph *Moon over Half Dome*. There are many mediums that bring nature to us within the comforts of our living rooms. Perhaps the deep spirituality we find in the outdoors is inspired by the sheer magnitude of canyon and sky, river and wind, that innate connection we feel to the ravens catching thermals overhead, the wildflowers spread out across the meadow—the awareness that we are part of something so much larger than ourselves.

Perhaps the spiritual richness is precipitated by the stark beauty of the wilderness, an awesomeness that is beyond description, leaving us standing on a promontory speechless, or gazing at a John Fielder photograph at a loss for words. Perhaps the spiritual door is opened by that feeling of smallness within the largeness. Out there we can no longer fool ourselves; ultimately it is not we who control the world. We wonder at the mystery of Creation, we marvel at the Creator. Or perhaps it is all of these elements building upon one another, generating a veritable cascade of spiritual opportunity.

How much easier it is for many of us to reach these spiritual heights in the wilderness than in a synagogue!

Bernice and Scott's Canyon trip was not an exception. As we hiked into the inner canyon, we hiked into our inner selves. We met each other in that inner chamber where true meeting is possible. When we gathered at the rim, the conversations were light. The students spoke about their majors, plans for after graduation, and their involvement in the outdoor club. But as we descended into the canyon, away from the protection of the tall Ponderosa pines, and into the exposure of the sparse juniper forest, the conversations deepened. We spoke of our hopes, dreams, disappointments, and doubts. What is it about the wilderness that makes us feel safe baring our souls to people we did not even know the day before?

They asked me what it was like being a rabbi. I told them what an honor it was to serve people and what joy I found from studying and living Jewishly. I told them about my congregation in Calgary, how stretched my time was, and how hard it felt sometimes to reach over the bimah, beyond the prayer book, past the office, and really reach people, and how confining I sometimes found the institution.

Then I asked them about being Jewish at college, and the stories tumbled out.

"I'm a Bu-Jew," Jen told me (a Jewish Buddhist). "I was raised Jewish, I even had a bat mitzvah, but I just can't buy the concept of a God who tallies up our rights and wrongs and then dishes out reward and punishment." She told me of her deep spiritual longing, her forays into yoga, Buddhism, and even Sufism.

Ben said, "The Canyon is my religion. I was raised Jewish, but I just don't like the way Judaism teaches us to have dominion over the earth. Besides, I never felt half as spiritual in temple as I do here. I think I might be a pagan." He spoke of magnificent moments he'd had on mountains, and about the community that forms as members of a group help one another to reach the summit. "I wish Judaism could be like that," he said.

Other students swapped stories about their boredom with Hebrew school, why kosher laws made no sense to them, how boring High Holidays were. One student raged about how a rabbi hadn't adequately been there for her mother when her grandmother had died. Her mother became a Unitarian, and then just stopped being involved in religion altogether. "We had never belonged to a congregation anyway," she said. "But that rabbi sort of sealed the deal." Another spoke with pain about a flippant comment a

Sunday school teacher had made ten years ago. She swore never to go back to synagogue and hadn't stepped foot in one since.

Most of the students had been to religious school until they turned thirteen. But they had never learned much about Judaism as adults, and their Jewish identity was mostly sustained by Chanukah latkes, Passover matzoh, and an occasional guilt-induced attendance at High Holiday services. Their occasional forays into Kabbalah had left them with red bracelets and a bitter emptiness. For them, spirituality and Judaism were as connected as Astroturf and Mozart.

These young men and women wanted a religion that was relevant, accessible, and spiritually nourishing. If they did not find it in Judaism, they would find it in Buddhism, paganism, or elsewhere. I realized that they had never had the opportunity to experience Judaism as I know it. They had not heard of the ancient rabbinical laws, from almost two thousand years ago, which teach us to be stewards of the earth, to protect it and guard it. "See to it that you do not destroy My world," says a sacred text written in the year 800 CE. It continues, "For if you do, there will be no one else to repair it" (Midrash Ecclesiastes Rabbah 1 on 7:13).

They had never stood on a mountain peak and said the words of the ancient biblical prayer the Shema, hearing it echo off the surrounding peaks, experiencing the oneness of all creation about which the prayer speaks.

They had never sat quietly by a river, meditating on the teachings of Martin Buber, our great Jewish philosopher, who taught that God is not an interventionist omniscient force, but rather that God is found in relationships, in the meeting of souls.

They had never climbed a 14,000-foot peak on the Sabbath and read the stirring words of Abraham Joshua Heschel. Rabbi Heschel taught that we access God through awe, by going to natural places, like the high peaks, which take us beyond the confines of words to that purely emotional and spiritual place that allows us to feel connected to something larger than ourselves.

It was not the students' fault that they had jettisoned their Judaism without ever really having the occasion to know it. Nature, which was once at the heart of Judaism, has been all but banished from our teachings.

Thousands of years ago, Jewish leaders tried to remove nature from Judaism. What were they so afraid of? That if people continued to worship on mountaintops they would not need the priests or large ornate temples? On top of mountains, the ancient Israelites could worship anywhere, anytime, but the high priests wanted to consolidate their power, so they built a huge temple in Jerusalem and taught that God wanted to be worshipped only within its walls.

Also our leaders were frightened by the seductiveness of paganism. Because Judaism grew out of pagan roots, the rabbis wanted to clearly differentiate monotheistic Judaism from its predecessor, paganism. They worried that if Jews continued to pray side by side with their pagan neighbors Judaism would slowly morph into the dominant religion of the time—paganism. The priests worried that the Jews might confuse being *inspired* by a mountain's beauty with worshipping the mountain *itself* as a god. With people spread all over, worshipping God on their own local mountaintop, there was no way to control the way in which the Jews practiced, and make sure that they did not veer into paganism. So the priests ordered the destruction of the altars on the high places and herded us all indoors.

But how do you do that? How do you change the way people have worshipped for centuries? In 622 BCE the priests of the Temple in Jerusalem made an incredible discovery. They found a fifth book of the Bible, and it contained just the passage needed. (I'm not sure how you find another book of the Bible, but maybe one morning a priest said, "I was pretty sure God had given us five books on Sinai, not just four. We should have a look around for it.") Turns out the book had been misplaced for a few centuries and fortunately, the priests found it—the book of Deuteronomy.

In an amazing coincidence, in the Book of Deuteronomy, God retracts an earlier pronouncement that *any* place can be holy. In Deuteronomy, God says high mountains, hills, and trees are no longer kosher for worship; rather all worship should be centralized in one spot—Jerusalem. In Deuteronomy chapter 12, God commands:

> You must destroy all the sites at which the nations you are to dispossess worshiped their gods, whether on lofty mountains and on hills or under any luxuriant. . . . Do not worship the Lord your God in like manner, but look only to the site that the Lord your God will choose amidst all your tribes as His habitation, to establish His name there. There you are to go, and there you are to bring your burnt offerings and other sacrifices, your tithes and contributions, your votive and freewill offerings, and the firstlings of your herds and flocks. (Deuteronomy 12:2, 4–6)

So, with this monumental discovery, coupled with the spread of literacy that enabled people to read the new book of the Bible, the people stopped worshipping on the high places, and the Temple became the center of Jewish practice, a tradition which has been passed on to the synagogues and churches of today. The distance between religion and nature had begun to grow.

And yet thousands of years later there I stood in the desert sand, a religious Jew, a rabbi no less, connecting Judaism and nature.

That night after we had made camp and cleaned up dinner, I made my way down to the river to sit by its edge. As I approached the great Colorado, I thought about how for millennia our people have sought out the spiritual awakening of rivers. Although today we believe God to be omnipresent, throughout the Bible God appears only at specific places at specific times. Most frequently, God appears near water, by trees, or on mountaintops. Other monumental experiences happen in those places as well.

One intriguing biblical story that takes place near a river is that of the patriarch Jacob, wrestling an adversary by the great river Yabok. His striving results in his new name, and that of the Jewish nation, Israel, sometimes translated as "God wrestlers." For thousands of years commentators have argued about who Jacob was wrestling. Was it an angel? God? Jacob's brother and longtime rival Esau? Did Jacob wrestle with himself, a conflict between the conniving man he had been and the loving patriarch he would become? The text can support all of these arguments. But what I find more compelling is the location—in the wilderness, by a river. Alone in the wilderness, isolated from family and friends, separated from his possessions, Jacob is finally able to face his adversary. Sometimes it takes the stark wilderness to help us face our truth and become our true selves. And so I believe it is not a coincidence that it is by the river Yabok, deep in the wilderness, rather than by an encampment or a city, that Jacob is given a new name, which will become the name of the Jewish nation, Israel. How fitting that several millennia later we would be naming the newest member of our tribe by a river!

As I stood in the dry desert by the powerful Colorado River, it was easy to imagine the holiness our ancestors attributed to water. They believed water flowed from a divine source, bridging the realms of God and humanity.

I sat down in the sand, feeling the heaviness of my exhausted legs. My body ached from the hike, and my heart ached for these Jews who do not know the Judaism I love so dearly.

How many Jews do we lose each year, because we do not share these teachings?

I listened to the sound of the massive Colorado River—surging, resting in eddies, charging over rocks—as it carved its way through the two-billion-year-old rock.

The sounds of the canyon reminded me of a story from our tradition about the great Rabbi Akiva. As a young adult, Akiva, who had no Jewish learning, sighted a rock that was being carved out by the slow, steady dripping of a spring. He thought to himself, "If water can carve out a rock, drip by drip, so too can I learn, letter by letter." He went immediately to start studying, learning the Hebrew letters—aleph, then bet—and years later he came to be known as one of our greatest scholars.

Just as rock and water taught Akiva, two thousand years ago, that it is never too late to start studying, the canyon holds lessons for us today. I heard the sharp nasal call of the nighthawk and the wheezy trill of the red-spotted toad, which have adapted to the desert heat and hunt only at night. So, too, I thought, Judaism can adapt and flourish. It is never too late to start, letter by letter, student by student.

The next morning we gathered by the water's edge to welcome Bernice and Scott's little girl into the covenant, to give her a name, and to bless her. We sat in a circle on the beach, beside a shallow eddy. We sang songs of welcome and gave thanks. We gave her the name Mariah, after the mountain in Israel, Moriah, where God spoke to Abraham, and where the great Temple was built. We prayed that our Mariah would experience the self-discovery and empowerment of climbing mountains and discover the peace and spiritual fulfillment that awaits us on the peaks. I also hoped that she would learn about the holiness of mountains and of temples.

We gave her the middle name Colorado, after the river. We prayed that like Jacob, who wrestled with God in the river, she too would wrestle with God concepts, finding one for herself. I hoped she would learn that there are many ways of thinking of God, and that she could be a good Jew even if she questioned God's existence.

I blessed her with ancient words from our texts, *Ye 'varehche'cha Adonai v 'yishm'rehcha*; May God bless you and keep you. Intertwined were the sounds, smells, and sights of the canyon. I prayed that she would gain the wisdom of a river, knowing which rocks to go around, which rocks to go over, and which to patiently carve through, drop by drop.

Then Bernice and Scott held Mariah Colorado close to them, and together father, mother, and daughter submerged three times in the river. This was the baby girl's mikvah, completing her conversion to Judaism.

That night by the campfire the Williams students said, "I've never seen religion like that. I didn't know it could be so relevant, so meaningful, so intertwined with nature. Tell me more."

For the next week, we hiked and talked. I shared with them Judaism as I experience it, a Judaism that does not insist on spending Saturday inside a synagogue but promotes the spirituality of the wilderness—and celebrates Sabbath while hiking, skiing, and biking. I introduced them to a Judaism with a strong environmental ethic. For example, the law of Ba'al Taschit, the prohibition against being wasteful, which today is known as "thou shalt recycle," and Tsa'ar Ba'alei Hayim, the law about kindness to animals. The non-Jews were excited by the conversation as well, saying, "I didn't know the Bible had concepts like that! Tell me more."

I told them that it is also Jewish to doubt whether or not God exists. For hundreds of years we have had theologies in which God is not a conscious force, controlling the world with puppet strings, but rather an energy force connecting all beings. They said, "That sounds like Buddhism. I didn't know Jews believed that! Tell me more."

We all left the canyon as different people. The Bu-Jew, the pagan, and several other students went on to study Judaism and reclaim their Jewish heritage. I still get e-mails from them, updating me on their journeys. I returned to Canada determined to continue combining the spirituality of the wilderness with Judaism. One verse kept going round and round in my mind, the very first verse of the Bible, "In the beginning, God created the heaven and the earth" (Genesis 1:1), and I thought to myself, "God started with sky and earth, not buildings, not churches or synagogues. How did so many of us manage to forget sky and earth?" I realized that there are many rabbis who can serve the 30 percent of American Jews who are affiliated with congregations, but how many rabbis are reaching the 70 percent who are not members of congregations? How many can relate to those who prefer skiing or hiking on Saturdays to attending a synagogue? How many rabbis are able to understand and accept those who say, "Running is my religion," or, "I feel more inspired reading Robert Frost poetry than Psalms"?

I put in my resignation from my congregation and in November 2001, I loaded my truck and drove back to the United States, this time to Boulder, Colorado, to launch the Adventure Rabbi program.

Adventure Rabbi? An oxymoron! Who ever heard of an adventurous rabbi! Yet here I am. On Adventure Rabbi trips we climb peaks, ride bikes, hike canyons, and ski the steeps, while we also attempt to reconnect with the ancient spirituality our ancestors experienced in the wild.

We pray, study text, debate, discuss, and wonder. We take traditional methods of Jewish teaching and discourse and transplant them into the wild, where somehow it is easier to speak one's heart, take risks, or explore new ideas with someone you have only just met.

How do you transform a day of powder skiing into a holy day? By stopping to notice a snow-dusted Douglas fir tree you might have skied by on another day. By learning the prayer for falling snow and teaching it to a friend. By sharing our dreams, hopes, and aspirations, rather than complaining about the pressures of work and stress in our overcommitted lives.

How do you turn a desert canyon into sacred space? By taking the time to really notice and appreciate the color of the sandstone and the smell of sage. By saying blessings combining traditional words with modern sentiments. By reading ancient words from a Torah, carried in a dry bag, and discussing how our own wilderness journey is similar to the journey our ancestors made.

And how can you find the solace of nature when the only canyons in your own backyard are those created by the shadows of skyscrapers? How can you bring the wilderness to the city? By heeding the ancient Jewish instruction to eat one of every type of each seasonal vegetable, in order to reconnect with the awe of Creation. By bringing a plant into your workspace and contemplating why the Talmud commands us to live only in cities that have natural spaces.

In short, I don't ask people to change their lifestyle, or insist that they give up treasured weekend days outdoors to go to synagogue. I challenge them to refocus their attention. "Your life is already spiritual," I say. "Let me show you how to make it Jewish."

One of the great rabbis, Rabbi Abraham ben Maimonides, taught: "In order to serve God, one needs access to the enjoyment of the beauties of nature, such as the contemplation of flower-decorated meadows, majestic mountains, and flowing rivers. For all these are essential to the spiritual development of even the holiest of people."*

In the pages that follow, we will explore why the natural world is essential to the spiritual development of Jews and Christians alike. Together we will walk through the pages of the Bible, visiting the places in which the Israelites met God in the wilderness. Some of the stories I am sure you will recognize—Moses and the burning bush, for example. Others may be less familiar. But each of these out-

---

*Rabbi David E. Stein, *A Garden of Choice Fruit* (Wyncote, PA: Shomreh Adamah, 1991), p. 68.

door meetings with God contains vibrant lessons for us, teachings that are unique because of the outdoor settings in which they were imparted. Although many of the messages have been ignored for centuries, ever since religion was moved into the confines of congregations, the lessons remain relevant and meaningful to our lives today.

What happened by those rivers and mountains, deep in the desert so many thousands of years ago? What was it our ancestors learned beneath the star-filled sky with the wind caressing their skin? What spiritual opportunities, what spiritual portals have we lost sight of by moving religion indoors?

Our ancestors experienced the spiritual connection between nature and religion, which many of us share. The sacred texts, so carefully preserved through the generations, contain clues about their ancient nature wisdom. Today we seek to retrieve the legacy of the ancient Israelites. Our journey reconnects the spirituality so many of us intuitively know exists in nature with its biblical roots.

Judaism and therefore Christianity began in the desert, by mountains and streams. Today we return to claim our inheritance.

# CHAPTER 1

# Cultivate the Patience to See Burning Bushes

*Moses said, "I must turn aside to look at this marvelous sight; why doesn't the bush burn up?" When the Lord saw that he had turned aside to look, God called to him out of the bush: "Moses! Moses!"*

—Exodus 3:3–4

Almost all of us know the story of the burning bush. Moses is out tending his father-in-law's flock when he notices an amazing sight—a bush that burns but is not consumed. He stops to look at it, and God appears to him from the flame. This is the first time that Moses meets God "face-to-face." God taps Moses as the man to free the Israelites and receive the Ten Commandments, and from there on, it's all history.

But what if the story had gone differently? What if it went something a little bit more like this: Moses is tending the flock of his father-in-law, Jethro, the priest of Midian. He drives the flock into the wilderness and comes to Horeb, the mountain of God. He had always found that place relaxing, although he never thought much about why, and since Moses has a lot on his mind this particular morning, he decides Horeb is, as always, a good place to sort through his thoughts.

Moses thinks through the day ahead. As soon as he has tended to the flock, he needs to rush back to the tent, change into his dress robes, and catch a caravan into the city, because he has a packed day of meetings ahead of him. He is trying to figure out how he can get all his work done in time to get to the gym that night, and still get home before his son Gershom goes to sleep, when his eye catches a marvelous sight! There is a bush all aflame, yet the bush is not being consumed by the fire. Moses says, "I must turn aside to look at this marvelous sight; why doesn't the bush burn up?"

Just then his cell phone vibrates. He grabs the phone out of his robe pocket. It is a text message from his friend Nathan, who always seems to know what is going on a few days before anyone else. Moses reads, "Wool futures 2 go up. Don't sell 2day. Call L8r. N8." By the time Moses has read the message, he is well past the bush and has already forgotten about the odd flames. With the phone still in hand, he calls his wife, Zipporah, just to check in.

Five minutes later, when he gets off the phone, he remembers the miraculous burning bush, but it is already well behind him. He thinks of going back but realizes that then he won't have time to stop for a cup of coffee, so he calls the fire department, which sends a crew to put out the fire.

Thus for a short time Moses became a local hero for saving the wilderness from burning down. Meanwhile, God tried the burning bush routine a few more times, but eventually God realized that no one had time to notice the subtle miracle and scribbled a quick note: "Note to Self: Command these people to take a day off every week so they have time to notice my miracles!" Then God switched to e-mail. But unfortunately, everyone thought God's messages were spam, and deleted them. So ends the story of the Israelites. The Bible never progresses past the burning bush scene of Exodus 3:3, well before the freeing of the Israelites from slavery, the parting of the Red Sea, and the awe-inspiring moment on Sinai, culminating with the giving of the Ten Commandments.

The rabbis teach us that the striking part of Moses' behavior in the burning bush story, in its original form, is that he takes the time to notice that the bush is burning but not being consumed. It takes patience to notice that something is on fire but not burning up, because you have to actually sit with it for a while to observe the changes, or lack thereof.

The Bible says, "When the Lord saw that he had turned aside to look, God called to him out of the bush" (Exodus 3:4), stressing that it is not until God sees that Moses turns aside that God actually speaks, as if this was the actual test. Will Moses notice? Will he take the time to stop and observe this peculiar sight?

Today our lives are so frenetic that, like Moses in the "what-if" version, we rarely have time to catch our breath, let alone be alert for spiritual portals or miracles. One of the reasons many of us love the desert is that when we are surrounded by the vast vistas, the sparse vegetation, and the bold colored rocks, we do have time to stop and notice. Out "there" we are able to remove ourselves from everything that normally demands our attention—e-mail, cell phones, voice mail, laundry, to-do lists, breaking news, not such breaking news, carpools, schedules, figuring out what we should make for dinner, and on and on. Perhaps the spirituality many of us experience outdoors is created by the simple fact that we are less distracted, so we are able to be deeply attentive to what is around us as well as what is inside us.

Throughout the Bible, theophany (God appearing to humans) does not occur just in the wilderness, but it usually does.* Perhaps God did try to show up in the towns or cities, but there was so much tumult—people coming and going, merchants hawking their wares, kids playing running games, friends shouting greetings—that no one noticed God.

One message of the burning bush story is that spiritual awareness involves slowing down and waking up to the world around us. I am not suggesting that if we slow down and take time to look, listen, and notice that we will actually meet God face-to-face, because according to Jewish tradition since the end of the prophetic age, God no longer makes direct contact with humanity.

But I believe we still have opportunities to meet the Divine (whatever you believe that to be), because in the wilderness, we connect with That Which Is Greater Than Ourselves (one of my favorite names for God), and we are embraced by a sense of belonging, of oneness, and of peace.

I know that it's not always possible (or even desirable) to relocate to the middle of the desert for a month. For people who live in the city, the closest you might get to the wilderness is an urban park. But even there you can cultivate the patience to see burning bushes and open yourself to spiritual opportunity. One of my favorite "tools" for

*Judges 13:2–3, Amos 7:4, Job 38:1 are all examples in which the location of the theophany is not specified, and in Exodus 40:34–38 and Numbers 10:35–36 the ark determines the location.

slowing down, taking notice, and being fully present is a short sensory meditation that can be done anywhere. Let me share with you how it worked on an Adventure Rabbi hike I was leading on the trails above Boulder, Colorado.

A group of forty people had gathered for one of our monthly Sabbath hikes. My task, in two hours, was to give the group a chance to separate from their workweeks, to slow down and catch up with themselves. Ultimately the goal was for them to taste "Sabbath rest."

There was a palpable buzz as we hiked up the trail—the excitement of people who were meeting for the first time and were not sure of what to expect. The steep red rocks ahead of us, jutting skyward above Boulder, had a luminous rosy glow to them, unique to the early-morning hours. The small wildflowers of early spring poked courageously from the still cold ground, and here and there pockets of snow still clung to the rocks. Early morning in Colorado is a glorious time for those who are awake!

As we hiked, I invited the group to try to consciously slow down their minds and shift into their "Sabbath souls," to allow themselves to experience the calmness and grace that surrounded us. As I listened to the talk on the trail, though, I realized that not only was the shift not happening but members of my group were not even noticing much of the natural scenery they were passing. Their workweeks were too entrenching, still demanding thought and attention, and their conversations with others on the trail were too compelling.

I stopped the group at a large rock outcrop, to try to readjust. As they sat down to rest, I read them the burning bush story. They immediately pointed out how hard it is to be like Moses today, to be fully present, to be here and now. Then we discussed how difficult it can be, even here in the outdoors, surrounded by nature, to stop our brain wheels from turning.

Then I introduced one of my favorite mind-focusing exercises, and the group agreed to try it. Each person would focus quietly on either listening or seeing for ten minutes, after which time we would share what we had noticed.

Ten minutes went by, uncomfortably at first and then, all of a sudden, too quickly. When the time was almost over, I slid my backpacker guitar out of my backpack. Quietly, I began to play "Oseh Shalom," a Jewish prayer for peace. Those who had wandered off to sit elsewhere made their way back to the rock, so that we were all sitting in a circle, and gradually the group joined me in song. Forty voices singing together, the ancient Hebrew words linking us together.

"So what did you notice?" I asked my now very chilled-out group.

"I noticed," said Greg, "how loud it was. I mean at first

when we stopped talking it was really quiet, but after a while I noticed all these sounds I didn't hear before, and it was really loud."

Kate said, "I hadn't heard a single bird while we hiked. But when I was quiet I heard chickadees, nuthatches and lots of bird sounds I didn't even recognize."

"I didn't realize how close we were to the road," said Steve. "It seemed so far away, but it was much louder than I thought it was."

The people who focused on the sense of sight during their ten minutes joined in.

Mark said, "At first I was disappointed that I had sat on the rock instead of in the meadow where all the flowers are. But after a while I noticed that there are several different lichens growing here, and the greens are all different, and quite beautiful."

"I was really taken by the textures. I was sitting under a ponderosa pine, and the bark falls off in these really cool patterns," said Anita.

David added, "I sat in the meadow and I was amazed at how many different types of grasses there are. I thought it would be just one kind of grass, but really there are quite a few."

Amazingly, we all seemed to share the experience "At first I thought one thing, but after I sat for a while I noticed something else." In order to be like Moses and truly notice what is directly in front of us, we learned that we needed to sit quietly for a while, to observe, and to become fully present.

As we continued up the trail, a feeling of tranquility permeated the group. Conversations shifted, and some people chose to hike silently. At last, most of us were fully present in the experience.

When we reached our destination, a natural sanctuary, we gathered in a circle and joined together in traditional Sabbath prayers. Then, after the last exhalation of sound had drifted over the foothills, we sat in silence for a long time. As I looked around the group, I saw that everyone's faces appeared less strained, and their shoulders had finally relaxed.

And as we hiked down the trail, I heard snippets of conversations: "What a difference it makes when you really slow down and notice what is around you!"

"That was the first time I've ever said a prayer and *felt* anything."

"I didn't know that Judaism could be so powerful."

"Too bad the congregation can't have their sanctuary up here! It would be so easy to pray!"

I privately gave thanks for this amazing trail, for rocks and flowers, for grasses and birds, for this experience that gave these forty people an opportunity to open their eyes, ears, and souls to the wonder of Creation. Their journey toward cultivating the patience to see burning bushes had begun.

I have repeated this simple yet powerful exercise countless times, seated and walking, outside and indoors. Although I love doing the exercise while hiking, it works indoors as well. I recently tried it with a group inside a sanctuary with wondrous results. What do you notice after gazing at your hand or listening to your own heartbeat for five minutes?

Heightened awareness is the first step toward engaging the spiritual possibility that continually surrounds us. It is accessible to us whether we live in Manhattan or Montana. Cultivate the patience to see burning bushes. You will be amazed at the wonders you discover. When we marvel at the world around us, we prepare to meet the miracles that await us, around most every corner.

# CHAPTER 2

# Take the First Step, the Sea May Part

*As the Israelites were departing defiantly, the Egyptians gave chase to them, and all the chariot horses of Pharaoh, his horsemen, and his warriors overtook them encamped by the sea . . .*

—Exodus 14:8–9

God's best, all-out, no-holds-barred miracle had to be the splitting of the Red Sea. In contrast with the burning bush, there was nothing subtle about this miracle. Just as Pharaoh's army is about to catch up with the Israelites and wipe them off the face of the earth, God parts the sea, allowing the Israelites to escape to the other side. Talk about God showing up at the right time, in the right place! This seaside appearance ranks number one on my list of top-ten miracles.

Do you ever wonder what happened to all the miracles? When I read the stories of the Bible, I sometimes think, "Why were there miracles then and not now? Couldn't God muster a little miracle today—to cure cancer or broker peace for Israel?" As Tevye asked in *Fiddler on the Roof,* "Would it spoil some big eternal plan?" For thousands of years, other people have read these same Bible stories and they too must have asked, "Why were there miracles then and not now? Has God deserted us? Where is God when we need a miracle?"

Theologians and other people who contemplate these sorts of questions offer us a variety of answers, including these: "The biblical miracles are myths to learn from. They didn't really happen." Or "In order for us to have free will, God can't intervene in our lives." Or "We don't deserve miracles from God. Our faith isn't strong enough."

So, if God doesn't do miracles anymore, why do we spend so much time learning about them? Perhaps there are other lessons embedded in the miracle stories that are still relevant and meaningful today. Let's take a closer look at one of the more well-known miracles of the Bible to see what we can uncover.

Many of us grew up watching Charlton Heston parting the Red Sea each spring when the movie *The Ten Commandments* was on TV, so you probably remember the story line.

After countless bargaining sessions with Moses, Pharaoh finally relented and acquiesced to God's demand: "Let My people go!"

Thus ended four hundred years of enslavement. Moses and his brother Aaron led the 600,000 men out of Egypt, with their women, children, flocks, and herds. Hastily, they set out across desert sands, triumphantly fleeing the taskmasters who had forced them to build Pharaoh's cities of Pithom and Raamses (Exodus 1:11). They were in such a hurry that they didn't even have time to let their bread rise, which is why Jewish people commemorate the exodus from Egypt each spring by eating unleavened bread called matzoh.

But barely a biblical chapter goes by before Pharaoh and his courtiers have a change of heart and wonder, "What is this thing we have done, releasing Israel from our service?" (Exodus 14:5). Pharaoh frantically sends off all his best chariots, along with the rest of his chariots (it really says that in the Bible!) and his horsemen and his warriors to pursue the bedraggled slaves.

The defenseless Israelites, camped down by the shores of the sea, are suddenly trapped between Pharaoh's oncoming army and the relentless waves of the sea. Certain that they are about to be driven into the sea by the oncoming Egyptian army, the people complain bitterly to God, "Why did you take us out of Egypt just to die in the wilderness?" They ask Moses, "Was it for want of graves in Egypt that you brought us to die in the wilderness?" (Exodus 14:11).

Moses reassures his frightened people, "Have no fear! Stand by, and witness the deliverance which the Lord will work for you today" (Exodus 14:13).

And then comes the great scene we all know so well. Moses raises his staff high in the air, and then "the Lord drove back the sea with a strong east wind all that night, and turned the sea into dry ground. The waters were split, and the Israelites went into the sea on dry ground, the waters forming a wall for them on their right and on their left" (Exodus 14:21–22).

But as the Egyptians gave chase, the waters closed back over them, drowning them, as the Israelites, reveling in their narrow escape, sang praises to God.

Even two thousand years ago the rabbis were concerned that people might erroneously conclude that the lesson this story teaches is that God will always be standing by ready to create miracles to save us. The ancient sages wanted to be sure we knew that although the Israelites had manna in the wilderness (the God-given food that sustained the Israelites during their wilderness trek), God no longer gives out free lunches. To clarify the meaning of the text, the rabbis wrote a Midrash, a text that explains the biblical text.

The rabbis explain that while the Israelites stood on the shore whining and complaining to God, one member of the tribe of Judah, Nachshon ben Aminadav, jumped into the sea. Only when he had walked in up to his nose and began to drown did God part the water (Michila d'Rabbi Yishmael Be Shalach, mesecta d'vay'hi parasha 5). So perhaps the story should read more like this:

The Israelites, trapped between Pharaoh's oncoming army and the Red Sea, complained bitterly to God and Moses, saying, "Was it for want of graves in Egypt that you brought us to die in the wilderness? What have you done to us, taking us out of Egypt?" (Exodus 14:11).

When the Israelites began to whine, might God have thought, "Oy! Enough already. All these people do is complain. I just freed them, not even a chapter ago, and they've already forgotten how powerful I am! They doubt that I can get them out of this pickle? I invented the pickle—kosher dill, sour, half-sour, even gherkins. At least I can count on Moses."

Meanwhile, Moses, having mastered the lesson of the burning bush, is busy observing the scene, noticing all the details, just as he learned. "Hmmm," he says. "There's a big, strong army approaching. Lots of dust, lots of chariots, lots of Pharaoh's men. Not so good. Over there is the cold, deep, and wide sea. Okay, there must be a burning bush around here somewhere that will tell me what to do."

God, listening to Moses, thinks, "It's enough that these Israelites whine all day. Can't Moses just step up to the plate for once and figure this one out? Do I always have to lay out everything for him? I can't be igniting the wilderness brush all the time! Enough is enough. Let them drown. I'll find myself a new people to give the Ten Commandments to."

Then God saw something that changed God's mind. Nachshon ben Aminadav, from the tribe of Judah, was walking away from the crowd, toward the sea. He had listened to the people's disgruntled complaints but did not join in. Instead, he turned away from the tumult and stepped into the water. Nachshon did not wait for Moses to tell him what to do or for God to give directions. He did not need to be reminded of all God had done for the people. Nachshon boldly stepped into the sea, not flinching even as the cold water spread over his sandals. He stepped in farther, the water now up to his ankles, and sank slightly into the sandy-loam bottom. He kept walking, the water rising up to his knees, his waist, and then up to his chest. He walked without hesitation until finally, when the water was at his nostrils and he began to gasp for air, God parted the Red Sea. Thus tradition teaches us that God parted the sea for Nachshon, who had dared to take the first step, and who was convinced that if he reached out to God, God would reach out to him.

The lesson the ancient sages who transmitted this story wanted us to learn is that we can't wait on the sidelines for God to rescue us. Rather we must be like Nachshon and take the first step. Only then will the sea part.

Most of us like to think of ourselves as Nachshon,

boldly stepping forward into the unknown. But there are many times when we are more like the Israelites, standing on the sidelines waiting for something to happen, for someone else to take care of the situation. Each of us has a little Nachshon and a little whiney bystander in us. Unfortunately, our cultural norm tends to be to dodge responsibility and claim, "That was his job, not mine," or, "It wasn't my responsibility to look after that." In the wake of the Hurricane Katrina disaster, for example, what did we see? On federal, state, and local levels of the government, just a lot of finger-pointing. "They were supposed to make sure the levees were safe," and "It was their job to orchestrate the evacuation."

When good things happen, we are quick to credit our own ingenuity or hard work, but when a bad thing happens we blame anyone and everyone else. Perhaps the extreme examples of this behavior are the lawsuits filed against fast-food restaurants blaming our obesity on their high-fat burgers and fries!

In stark contrast, in the wilderness we can't expect anyone to take care of us. Rather part of the thrill of outdoor adventure is knowing that everything you need must be carried on your own back. If you forget to pack it before you leave the comforts of civilization, you simply will have to figure out how to do without it in the backcountry. Nature, thus, is a great training ground for becoming more like Nachshon.

When I am thirsty in the wilderness, there is no faucet to turn on. I carry all my water on my back and plan my route so that I cross streams to replenish my supply. When I am cold, there is no thermostat to adjust. Rather I put on a jacket and hat or hike more quickly.

Perhaps God decreed that the Israelites would spend forty years in the desert before they were permitted to enter the Promised Land in order to learn about self-sufficiency. As slaves, they were not allowed to think or do for themselves. But the next generation, born into freedom in the wilderness, would grow up learning how to take care of themselves and each other, and would know how to accept and share responsibility, rather than always whining to God and Moses.

Fortunately, we can practice these skills on a day hike or on a weeklong wilderness trip, rather than a forty-year desert trek.

For years I have taught the Nachshon story on the trips I guide. I always thought that the ending provided a powerful teaching, until something took place on a trip and the story stopped making sense to me. This often happens when studying the Bible. At first, the story or lesson seems simple enough, but then if you study a passage long enough, eventually it stops making sense until a new nuance of meaning presents itself.

Scholar ben Bag-Bag, who lived two thousand years ago, in the first century, and was considered to be a great expert on the Bible, explained this experience quite well. (He is frequently quoted, and I often wonder if it is because he was so wise or because his name is so much fun to say!) Ben Bag-Bag wrote in the Mishnah, "Turn it, and turn it, for everything is in it. Reflect on it and grow old and gray with it" (Pirke Avot 5:22). In other words, study the Bible over the course of your entire life. As you grow older, you will look at it differently and you will discover new facets to each teaching. (Or could he mean that the more you study, the more the meanings will shift and you will grow gray with frustration trying to figure it out?)

Many years ago I too had a "ben Bag-Bag meets Nachshon" experience. I was leading a backpacking trip in the Cascade Mountains of Washington State. The Cascades can best be described as, well, wet. It rained every day, and the vegetation was lush, the wildflowers abundant, and the rivers . . . Oh, what rivers!

On the first day, it was already apparent that I needed to get the group mentally prepared for the many difficult river crossings we would face. That evening, as our pot of macaroni and cheese bubbled on the camp stove, I pulled my Bible out of my pack and read the group the story of the Israelites' crossing of the Red Sea. Next I told them the Nachshon story. We had nine more days of river crossings in front of us, and I hoped they might find inspiration in our common ancestors' bold first step, a step that caused the sea to part.

We talked about using the trip to develop our inner Nachshons, to literally practice taking the first step across rivers. Then we expanded on the metaphor. Could crossing the rivers help us learn to take the first step in our lives, leaving a job, starting a new relationship, expanding our hobbies? We also wondered what enables us to step forward and what holds us back. Fear of failure? Lack of skills? Complacency? We wondered which restraints are real and which ones we fabricate.

The very next day we were at a particularly rough river crossing. The river flowed through a tight valley, which compressed the water into a narrow, swift, and deep channel. The water charged through rapidly, voraciously eroding the banks into steep slopes. As I stood at the edge looking down, my breath caught in my chest as I watched the power of the churning water below.

Fortunately, there was a log that had fallen across the river that we could use as a bridge. The log was old and thick, and its bark was covered with moss that was wet and slick. The crossing would demand complete focus, but I was sure it was doable. One by one we crossed, each person shouting, "Nachshon!" as he or she took the first step out onto the log and then crossed to the other side.

But then it was Lee's turn. She too cried, "Nachshon!" and took the first step and a second. But then she stopped.

"Come on, Lee," I said. "Keep on moving. Use your momentum to cross the river."

But she didn't budge. She stood on the log, looking down at the water churning below, and she froze in her tracks.

"Are you okay, Lee?" I asked.

"I'm not going out there," she said. "I took my steps. Now I'm waiting right here for the miracle. I'm waiting right here until the sea parts."

That was, after all, what the Nachshon story promised. "Take the first step and the sea will part." Now what? I scrambled up onto the log behind her and helped her slowly ease her way across the log, saying, "Okay, next foot here, next foot there, keep your weight low. You can do it." Meanwhile our group, half on each bank, shouted words of encouragement, "You can do it, Lee. We know you can!"

Eventually, she did cross the log. But in the moment that Lee froze on the log, saying, "I took my steps. Where's my miracle?" I had my ben Bag-Bag moment. In that second I understood that there was a basic flaw in the way I had taught the Nachshon story. Lee had turned the teaching over, and it had stopped making sense to me. Since Judaism teaches that the age of miracles is over and God no longer intervenes in our daily lives, what are we stepping toward, if not toward God's miracle?

For years I had taught, "Take the first step, the sea will part." But Lee could have waited all day and God would not have reached down to transport her to the other side. So what kind of miracle can we expect, if any?

The truth is that there are no capital-*M,* God-reaching-down-from-heaven Miracles anymore. But there are small-*m,* humans-doing-incredible-things miracles. Perhaps the miracle on our backpacking trip was simply that once Lee took the first step, she was able, with coaching and encouragement, to take the next step, and the next, and the next. It's like a *Wizard of Oz* moment. As with the Lion, the Tin Man, and the Scarecrow, the miracle was when Lee realized she had the ability inside her all along to cross the log. Sometimes it takes coaching and encouragement, but that is another small-*m* miracle. We have friends, family, and teachers who support us.

And last but not least, self-discovery is the miracle that enables each of us to do what needs to be done in the world. If we can take that first step, then even if we are scared, or uncertain, we can still make it across the metaphorical rivers of life, such as leaving an unhealthy relationship, learning to dance, or moving to a new city.

Have you ever been in a situation where you just couldn't see a solution and then you did something, anything, and suddenly the solution appeared? Taking the first step enables doors to open for us. Possibilities unfold that we could not see from our previous vantage point. I don't mean to imply that each of us has a destiny and that when we take the first step it will unfold. I do not believe in pre-ordained destiny, or that each of us has a set role in life. But

I do believe that each of us has myriad options, and the more steps we take, the more options will unfold for us.

Here is one of my pivotal stories of how taking that first bold step changed the direction of my life.

After serving as a rabbi in Canada for several years, I was eager to move back to the United States. I wanted to move back to Colorado, but there were no job openings there, so I interviewed for positions all over the country, including St. Louis, Boston, and San Diego. Several of the positions seemed promising. They were with growing congregations, with exciting programs, nice financial packages, and wonderful teams of colleagues. Yet despite all they promised, I could not quite bring myself to accept an offer. My friends said, "That is an awesome job! Take that one." Or, "You'll love Boston. What a great town!" But each time I picked up the phone to call the congregational president and say, "Thank you! Yes, I would love to come work for you," I put the phone down and went for a trail run instead.

I was torn because despite the merits of each congregation, none was in Colorado. Any of them would satisfy my first priority of returning home to the United States; but I wasn't convinced that my soul could thrive if I continued to live in a city.

In the middle of this turmoil, my friend Rhonda invited me over for a swim in her lake. After swimming, we lay on the wooden dock, which had grown warm from hours of baking in the midmorning sun. I told Rhonda about the job search and she said, "I don't think you're going about this right. You're looking for jobs, not places to live. That works for some people. But for you, where you live, being near nature, is too important. You should pick the place and then find a job."

I assured her that she was wrong, because that was just not how it was done in the world of clergy. "You don't just pick up and move somewhere. There are only so many positions, after all." But later that day when I was out riding my bike, I thought about what she said. I thought and thought and thought and thought until finally I realized she was right. Within twenty-four hours I had turned down all the job offers, and not long after that I rented a one-way U-Haul truck, packed up my belongings, and moved to Colorado.

It was November 2001 when I drove across the U.S. border and settled in Boulder, Colorado. I had no job, and some of my colleagues thought I was crazy. With such great job offers, why make such a foolhardy move? But I took that step into the unknown.

I arrived with no job, and limited savings, but I had a unique opportunity to think about what I really wanted to do with my life. I asked myself question after question. What am I really passionate about? What do I really believe in? And inspired by the work of author Jim Collins, what do I love to do, that I am good at, that I can make a living at, and that will make the world a better place?

I did a lot of hiking, running, yoga, biking, and skiing and a lot of thinking. I spent hours and hours outdoors, where I do my best thinking, and where I could practice taking bold steps by jumping rock spans and crossing rivers. And within four months of my arrival, I started the Adventure Rabbi program. Running a Jewish outdoor adventure program had been a pipe dream of mine since my trip into the Grand Canyon to officiate at Mariah's conversion ceremony the year before. When deep in the canyon the Williams students had dreamed up the name "Adventure Rabbi" and proposed the concept of my leading Jewish outdoor adventures, I didn't think it was realistic. Now, suddenly, from my new vantage point, it became a possibility. I didn't know it would work when I launched the program, but I had a dream that, if nothing else, was worth a try. I was lucky to have friends and family standing on the sidelines encouraging me, just as I had encouraged Lee across that log. They helped me understand that even if the idea flopped, if I failed and fell in the river, that, too, was okay. At least I would have tried.

With each step, each engaged couple who wanted me to officiate at their mountaintop wedding, each group I took on a Sabbath hike, each religious school class I took up a mountain, other possibilities presented themselves. Soon there was an Adventure Rabbi Web site with a social networking program, linking a virtual community spanning states and countries, and giving people the opportunity to explore ideas, ask questions, and find like-minded individuals.

As my dream became reality and the organization grew, one online newsletter sign-up at a time, each step emboldened me to take the next. But had I not taken that first step of moving to Boulder, I imagine my dream may not have come to fruition. And so I ask: What rivers are you ready to cross? What do you need to do to allow yourself to take that first step?

Maybe it's time to brush up your résumé and take a look at what jobs are opening up in your field. Or take a cooking class and throw dinner parties that wow your friends and enhance your social life. Maybe have a look at the procedures and requirements for adopting a baby from overseas. Maybe start researching and saving up for that vacation you've been dreaming about for years.

Whatever your river is, may you have the courage to take the first step and then discover the ability to take the next, and the next, and the next, as the lowercase-*m* miracles unfold around you.

# CHAPTER 3

# Rediscover Awe

*Now Mount Sinai was all in smoke, for the*
*Lord had come down upon it in fire; the smoke*
*rose like the smoke of a kiln, and the whole*
*mountain trembled violently.*

—Exodus 19:18

Did you ever wonder why God makes Moses climb Mount
Sinai to get the Ten Commandments? Wasn't there a nice
desert oasis where they could meet? Or if they needed more
privacy than an oasis could offer, why couldn't God have just
said, "Psst, Moses, over here behind the sand dune"?

I asked this question to a group of rabbinical students I
was training, as I led them on a relentless hike up Green
Mountain, whose peak towers over Boulder. Evon, as
much out of breath as his classmates, answered, "Because
God figured Moses would be so out of breath that he

wouldn't be able to say, 'No thanks,' and not accept the Commandments."

What I was looking for was something more like "Because when you work for something it means more to you." Or "Because there were fewer distractions on a mountain and Moses could really focus." But the more I thought about it, the more I liked Evon's answer.

Perhaps God did make Moses climb Mount Sinai to receive the Ten Commandments so that Moses would move beyond the confines of words. The physical exertion of the desert climb, coupled with the stark desert beauty, helped Moses to arrive spiritually and emotionally in a place beyond internal chatter, a place beyond rationalization or explanation. A state often called awe, in which you open your mouth to describe what is happening and find the only thing you can say is "Wow." Only in this state was Moses able to hear the word of God, to sense God's presence, to reach out to the Divine.

Ironically then, although the Mount Sinai story is all about the words that were given there, it is also about an experience that is beyond words.

Rabbi Abraham Joshua Heschel, one of our great contemporary thinkers, taught about awe saying, "God begins where words end."* He believed that awe, surely what

---

*Abraham Joshua Heschel, *Man Is Not Alone* (New York: The Noonday Press, 1951), p. 98.

Moses experienced on Sinai, is a prerequisite for the contemplation of God.

What is awe? Awe is the ineffable emotion we experience when we step outside the realm of humanity and realize the mystery of the universe. Awe is the inexpressible feeling we have when witnessing the birth of a child, a thunderstorm rolling over the plains, or a peregrine falcon soaring above a jagged cliff. Awe is the realization that we exist.

This is what awe feels like to me. I stand on top of a mountain, unable to describe in mere words the feeling of standing on a peak, the wind blowing against my face, as I look out across the world from a vantage point of 14,000 feet. How can I describe the feeling of sheer power, the exhilaration after climbing for hours and hours? Of standing on the heights above where the birds soar, powered to the top by my own muscles, now taut with exertion?

And at the very same time, it is impossible to avoid feeling powerless. Standing at the summit peak, surrounded by the vast stretches of wilderness, it's hard not to ask, "Of what worth is my small life in this large and complex world?"

Conveying this feeling of such smallness, yet such absolute connection to something greater than myself, is no easy task. I am rapt in a cascade of emotions, an experience that is beyond words; it is awe.

Moses' Sinai experience was perhaps the most awesome moment in the Bible. Here is how I imagine the scene as I read the text:

Thunder roared. Flashes of lightning illuminated the sky. The Israelites were frightened; surrounded by the stunning noises of thunder crashing, flames of fire flaring, and rocks sliding, smashing, and shattering—they stepped back and would climb no farther. But at the shores of the Red Sea Moses had learned the lesson of taking the first step, so he knew that he must climb on and reach toward God if he wanted God to reach toward him. Moses climbed the mountain, step by step, until he stood atop the craggy desert peak, its red rocks jutting upward toward heaven. Surrounding the mountain was the vast and stark desert. The wilderness stretched out to the north, to the south, to the east, and to the west, seemingly forever.

As the mountain trembled, Moses braced himself against a rock on the summit, listening and watching. A dense cloud hovered over the peak, and within it Moses waited. His strong, weatherworn body was silhouetted on the rock by the red flashes of fire and thick plumes of smoke that emanated from the summit.

Then, finally, the Voice thundered across the vast desert, echoing through the wilderness. God commanded, "Thou shall not murder. . . . Thou shall not steal" (Exodus 20:13). (JB)

And so it was that Moses received the Ten Commandments from God. He then descended from the mountain heights to give God's commandments, engraved on stone tablets, to the Israelites, who through the centuries have learned from them, lived by them, and died for them. They have held them in their hearts and souls, passing them from generation to generation. These heavy stone tablets, and the laws and the stories that surround them, introduced a monotheistic, ethics-based religion and therefore changed the course of history.

Despite the palpable role of nature in the revelation, despite the crucial role the natural environment served in moving Moses to a place of awe, for thousands of years we have been taught to focus on the words that were given, rather than the place in which they were given. The actual mountain, we are told, is unimportant. Why would religious leaders negate such an important factor of the Mount Sinai experience? Jewish tradition teaches that God didn't want us to focus on the particular place or revelation, lest it become a religious shrine and a tourist attraction. These are good reasons, yet is it possible that we lost a crucial part of the revelation when we left the mountain behind?

It is shocking that immediately after this intense moment of awe, of meeting God on a *mountain*, Moses charges down to the valley with God's instructions for the people to build a Tabernacle, a place for the Israelites to meet God indoors. God commanded, "And let them make Me a sanctuary that I may dwell among them" (Exodus 25:8). Thus the age of indoor religion began. The Tabernacle became the Temple in Jerusalem, which was the model for our churches and synagogues of today. How different religion might have been had we kept the wilderness tradition of awe alive!

Instead, for thousands of years we have viewed the study of the Ten Commandments and the Bible, which many say was also given at Sinai, as our primary pathways to God. Through the centuries we have built countless houses of worship, so that we can gather in community and study God's sacred words. We pray together in comfortable sanctuaries, protected from the elements. We have long forgotten to wonder what spiritual opportunities we may have lost by moving indoors. Collectively, we have disregarded the underlying experience of the mountain itself.

And yet it is clear that we left something critical behind when we moved indoors. Consider the myriad ways indoor-based religions strive to re-create the sense of awe we had on Sinai. For example, religious buildings are constructed with awe in mind. Think about the massive, cathedral-like sanctuaries built by the early Reform Jews in America in the late 1800s and early 1900s. Much like their neighboring Christian houses of worship, these supersized structures with their vaulted ceilings, pillars, and elaborate stained-glass windows were designed to invoke that feeling of awe we experience so easily in nature. Architects have attempted to re-create the feeling of smallness within something larger, of marvel and inspiration.

Ironically, though, this feeling of awe is lost on most of us today because when we walk into such a space we tend to think things like, "Wow, it must cost a bundle to heat this place in the winter." We then turn down the hall and look for a more intimate, cozy worship space in which to pray.

The blessings and rituals that surround the reading of the Bible in its original Hebrew text are also designed to invoke feelings of awe, and to re-create the experience of Sinai. As the cantor sings out in a strong, stirring voice, the congregation rises to their feet. The rabbi opens the doors of the ark, the focal point of the sanctuary, positioned high above the congregation. The open doors reveal the sacred scrolls, covered in gold-embroidered velvet and adorned with silver ornaments.

Lifting the Torah scroll high into the air, the rabbi then carries the handwritten Hebrew words of the Bible through the congregation as everyone watches and sings, and reaches out to touch the Torah. The rabbi then ascends the stagelike platform called the bimah (the biblical word for "high place"). Prayers are offered, and then the Bible reading commences, the timeless, ancient chant of words given to us millennia ago at Sinai.

For many of us, this is an awe-inspiring moment, re-connecting us to the Sinai experience. The room vibrates with the ancient melodies as the Torah reader sings out words that our people have chanted for generations. The moment transcends time and connects us with the generations who have preceded us, as well as the generations who will follow.

But others seated at the same service are counting the pages until the service will be over, and wondering why there is so much standing, sitting, and standing again. They wonder, "What does all that Hebrew mean, and what does it have to do with today?" And sometimes, even if someone understands the Hebrew that is being chanted, participating is at best an intellectual exercise. The skillfully written sermon of the rabbi may make it relevant, and meaningful. But awesome? Not so much.

Frankly, sometimes words are not enough. Sometimes the words even get in the way of finding spirituality.

Rabbi Heschel taught that there are three different pathways to awe, and therefore to meeting the Divine. He wrote, "There are three starting points of contemplation about God; three trails that lead to Him. The first is the way of sensing the presence of God in the world, in things; the second is the way of sensing His presence in the Bible; the third is the way of sensing his presence in sacred deeds (mitzvot)."*

The second and third, the study of the Bible and the doing of sacred deeds, are zealously pursued by organized religion. Mount Sinai represents the first (and all too often

*Abraham Joshua Heschel, *God in Search of Man* (New York: The Noonday Press, 1955), p. 31.

forgotten) pathway to awe, sensing the presence of God in the world.

Rabbi Heschel wrote, "It is only when we suddenly come up against things obviously beyond the scope of human domination or jurisdiction, such as mountains or oceans, or uncontrollable events like sudden death, earthquakes or other catastrophes, that we are somewhat shaken out of our illusions [that we are in charge]."* And he writes, "Confined in our own study rooms, we may entertain any idea that comes to our minds. Under such circumstances it is even plausible to say that the world is worthless and all meaning a dream or fiction. And yet, no one can sneer at the stars, mock the dawn, ridicule the outburst of spring, or scoff at the totality of being. Away from the immense, cloistered in our own concepts, we may scorn and revile everything. But standing between heaven and earth, we are silenced."†

I submit that in a typical religious setting, there are two stumbling blocks between us and awe. First, not all people will connect with God through studying the Bible, worshipping, or doing sacred deeds. Today, 70 percent of the Jews in America are not affiliated with a congregation. We need to open the doors of our synagogues and churches and walk outside to reclaim the pathway of "sensing the pres-

---

*Heschel, *Man Is Not Alone,* p. 290.
†Heschel, *God in Search of Man,* pp. 105–6.

ence of God in the world."* After all, "in the world," not in the synagogue, is where 70 percent of the people are!

Obviously, I think the location of the giving of the Commandments, the mountain, was a critical element of Moses' experience. As I discuss throughout this book, nature offers many of us the most propitious opportunity to rediscover awe and reconnect with God. Even now, sitting at my desk and looking out the window, the opportunity for connection awaits me. Last night's storm has covered the backyard in a blanket of snow, still undisturbed by our footprints. The snowflakes glitter like diamond dust as they catch the rays of the early-morning sun. On the south side of the house, I watch drops of water sliding down a precariously long icicle. What a potent spiritual springboard we neglect when we cloister ourselves indoors in windowless sanctuaries or behind stained-glass windows.

The second stumbling block is cultural. In our jet-set, Internet era of scientific discovery, technological advancement, extreme sports, and adventure collecting, we are "overawed." All too often when we confront awesome situations, we don't even notice them. As our knowledge and control of nature increases, the mystery of the world decreases. How awesome is a sunrise if you focus on the mechanics of the earth's 24.5-degree rotation pattern?

We are exposed to so much that is incredible—the

*Heschel, *God in Search of Man*, p. 31.

"little-*m*" miracles we discussed earlier—that now hardly anything seems incredible. We can take pictures of planet Earth from space and we can pop a pill that can cure an infection. We take such wonders for granted. What a loss! So what is required for us to arrive at a place beyond words? How can we truly feel awe in any situation? We must recalibrate our awe meters, so we can genuinely experience awe once again.

It saddens me when I take a group up a peak to experience the spiritual portals opened by awe, and they say, "It's a lovely view, but awesome? A place beyond words? Spiritually transformative? Not really."

Children instinctively understand awe. I remember when my daughter, Sadie, first noticed her hand and her tiny fingers that she could move all by herself, and a few weeks later, when she could lift and turn her head, she noticed that there was an entire world behind her, not just in front of her. You and I also had moments just like this when we were infants. How much we have forgotten! We once experienced awe everywhere we looked.

When Sadie was about eighteen months old, she discovered the moon. Even today at bedtime she still runs to the window and calls, "Let's look for the moon!" When we can spot it she cries, "Oooooo!" as if she had never seen the moon before. Each night she experiences anew the wonder of the waxing and waning white moon. When we come to life from a perspective of awe, this is how we experience the world. The spiritual practice of experiencing awe can begin with recalibrating your awe meter until seeing the moon from your bedroom window is almost as spiritually powerful as seeing it from atop a peak in the Rocky Mountains, or looking at your own hand can once again evoke a sense of wonder.

Here is another piece of the puzzle. The Bible gives us very little information about Mount Sinai. There are no geographic landmarks, no latitude and longitude. Admittedly those measures hadn't been invented yet, but the Bible still could have said something like "Sinai is the third mountain to the north of the tall one." Consequently, despite claims to the contrary, we do not even know for certain which mountain *is* Sinai.

The Midrash builds on this paucity of detail, teaching that Mount Sinai was not the largest peak in the area. It was not even very majestic. It was really just a little peak.* Imagine, the place in which the Israelites experienced God's presence and received the Ten Commandments, the laws that came to shape our society today, was a small, unremarkable peak. The lesson? If your awe meter is properly calibrated, you don't have to climb Everest to reach spiritual heights. You can go for a walk up the street or climb the Great Hill in the north part of Central Park and still experience awe.

---

*Louis Ginzberg, *Legends of the Jews* (Philadelphia: The Jewish Publication Society, 2003), pp. 594–96.

Rediscovering awe and recalibrating your awe meter begin with opening your eyes and ears to your surroundings. Bring nature into your home and office and allow it to open the doorway for you. Buy a house plant. Move your desk so that you look out a window. Change the route you take to work so that you drive through or around a park. Walk around the block after dinner. Notice what the clouds are doing. Learn to recognize the moon's phases. Get in the habit of pointing things out to yourself and to others. See how that branch of blossoms lies so gracefully over the other? How proud that robin looks walking across the grass?

In the beginning, these "beauty alerts" may simply be natural oases brought into your day. But cumulatively they build into a spiritual practice that can allow you to access the awe of Sinai, even when you are simply sitting at your kitchen table looking at an African violet in bloom.

When I am in Manhattan I always try to walk across Central Park, even if it takes a few minutes longer to get where I am going. The moment I enter the park, I feel an immediate shift in my being, as if sensing soil beneath my feet, instead of concrete, reconnects me with that universal energy that connects all beings. While in Central Park recently I came upon a grove of elm trees. Their intertwining branches danced in the light wind that blew through the park. Elm is a species that has been decimated in many parts of the country by Dutch elm disease. When I was a natural resources undergraduate at Cornell University, my professors used to say that before the disease, a tall stand of elm trees lined the main street leading in to campus; the elm were tall and proud and delightfully shady. But I had never seen them, and could only imagine that elm trees could be that impressive. Now years later when I came upon a grove of elm so unexpectedly, my soul soared to see the tall, upward yearning of their majestic branches, spared from the ravages of the disease. They were, indeed, inspirational.

What makes your soul soar? Train yourself to look for moments when you see something that causes you to shift to a place of connection, of peacefulness. How can you bring that more frequently into your life? When can you make time in your life to notice? Perhaps the Sabbath? Listen for moments that make your soul sing and your heart open. The daffodils poking out of the warmed soil in the small garden strip in front of your supermarket? Children exploring a stream bank? The puzzle pattern of the bark on a sycamore tree?

Frankly, I don't believe any of us will ever climb a mountain and hear the voice of God. But we will experience awe as we connect with "That Which is Greater than ourselves." Awe allows us to feel part of the Divine energy that courses through the universe. That place of awe, from which our contemplation of God begins, awaits us in the nooks and crannies of the natural world. Therefore we must seek them out, soak them in, and care for them.

# CHAPTER 4

# Remember Sabbath Rest:
# Fourth on God's Top Ten List

*Remember the sabbath day and keep it holy. Six
days you shall labor and do all your work, but
the seventh day is a sabbath of the Lord your
God: you shall not do any work . . .*

—Exodus 20: 8–9

The Sabbath is one of the greatest gifts that the Jews have
given the world. I'm not suggesting that the entire Ten
Commandments aren't stellar or that they didn't make a
splash. But number four on God's Top Ten list, the command to take a day off, radically changed the world.

Before God gave us the Ten Commandments, people
worked seven days a week, without rest. With the advent
of the Sabbath, the Bible presented a revolutionary idea.
Not only should men have a day off, but women, children,

slaves, and even cows should take part in this weekly day of rest.

It's a good thing the idea came from God, because employers probably would have said, "You want a day off? Once a week??? I don't think so. Now get back to work!"

Number four, "Remember the sabbath and keep it holy," ranks ahead of "You shall not murder" (number six), and "You shall not steal" (number eight). Clearly we are supposed to take Sabbath rest seriously. Imagine if we lived in a society that believed that working seven days a week was as heinous a crime as murder or theft!

I've noticed that many of us unconsciously divide the Ten Commandments into two groups. In the first group are the commandments that seem like obvious, good rules for any society. "Don't steal" and "Don't murder" fall into this category. They seem so obvious that the Ten Commandments don't even get much credit for them anymore.

The second group includes the commandments that we just sort of ignore. These are the commandments that seem irrelevant in our society, that we don't understand, or that we just don't want to think about. Observing the Sabbath seems to fall in this group—it's one of the ones you can't quite remember when you are trying to recall all ten of the commandments.

For example, what does this mean? "You shall not take the name of the Lord your God in vain; for the Lord will not hold him guiltless who takes his name in vain" (Exodus

20:7). (Soncino) Many of us erroneously think that this means that we shouldn't use God's name in a curse, as in "goddamn, that car just cut me off!" or that we have to write out God like this: "G-d." But what the original Hebrew actually commands is don't "carry" God's name in vain, meaning don't use God's name to justify your own causes. God doesn't want you to sully God's name for your personal agenda.* I can think of a few "religious" people who could use a refresher course on the meaning of this commandment! And for most all of us, this one goes in group number two.

And how about this one? "You shall have no other gods before me. You shall not make for you any graven image, or any likeness of any thing that is in heaven above, or that is in the earth beneath, or that is in the water under the earth" (Exodus 20:3–4). What is a "graven image" anyway? We often think this just means don't make any images of God. But look closely and that's not what it says; it says don't make images or likenesses of *anything* in heaven, on earth, or in the water. If we want to follow this one, we better quickly start culling our art collections. Most likely, this command was a polemic against paganism, created out of fear that people would make sculptures and pictures of, for example, fish, trees, and birds and then might be com-

---

*Rabbi Joseph Telushkin, *Jewish Literacy* (New York: William Morrow and Company, 1991), p. 56.

pelled to pray to them. So the painting of the Grand Canyon, which I mentioned at the beginning of this book and which instigated the creation of the Adventure Rabbi program, might need to go out in the trash heap if I were going to heed this commandment. This commandment also goes in category two.

And does this one really apply to us? "You shall not covet your neighbor's house; you shall not covet your neighbor's wife, or his male or female slave, or his ox or his ass, or anything that is your neighbor's" (Exodus 20:14). How about my friends Andy and Katherine's Toyota Prius Hybrid? The Bible doesn't say anything specifically about not coveting cars, although I suppose it is implied. But on the other hand, since the Prius is good for the environment, doesn't that cancel out my coveting?

So what about the Sabbath? I mean, who really has time to take twenty-four hours off every week? Especially now that I have added to our to-do lists: look for burning bushes, take the first step, and rediscover awe. We are really busy people! So, not surprisingly, many of us sort of skip this one, or at least don't take it as seriously as "You shall not murder."

But I would like to see the Sabbath commandment re-designated to group number one—the group for obvious good rules for any society. Taking a day off once a week to connect with family, friends, yourself, and God (whatever that means to you) may well be among the most spiritually important lessons the Bible has to teach us.

Our lives are like run-on sentences as we get up, check e-mail, grab breakfast, go to work, meet friends for lunch, get back to work, instant message (IM), check e-mail, rush to the gym to do a quick workout, shower, drop off the dry cleaning, pick up dinner, IM, check e-mail, eat dinner, IM, clean the kitchen, go to sleep, remember to call your mother back, call your mother, now really go to sleep. And then we wake up in the morning to do it all again.

Here is a conversation I hear a lot. Does it sound familiar to you? "How *are* you?" you ask your friend. "Good. Busy," he answers. "Busy, but good." In our culture, being busy is a badge of honor and a source of pride. A full schedule means we're working and playing hard. We are achievers, not slackers. If workdays and weekends are busy, it means we are experiencing life to its fullest. We are not missing out. We are living. Who needs time for a day off?

Our frenetic lifestyles may seem like a new thing, but really they are as old as the Bible itself. Even back then people had to be commanded to take a day off or they would just work, work, work. Why else would God have made a day off one of the Ten Commandments?

Moses, for example, may have been a great prophet, but when it came to work-life balance, he did not have it figured out either. God's number one man of the Five

Books was a workaholic through and through! When Moses was preparing to lead the Israelites on their forty-year trek through the desert, for example, he had so little time for family that he sent his wife and sons to live with his wife's family in another part of the desert. In hindsight, maybe the trip would not have taken quite so much of his time if he had had his wife's counsel. Maybe she could have convinced him to stop and ask for directions!

Eventually, though, Moses' father-in-law, Jethro, brings Moses' wife and sons back to Moses in the desert and tells his son-in-law to get his act together. Jethro insists that Moses delegate some of his work because otherwise, he tells Moses, you will be no good to anyone. The Bible describes the scene, "But Moses' father-in-law said to him, 'The thing you are doing is not right; you will surely wear yourself out, and these people as well'" (Exodus 18:17–18). Fortunately for all of us, Moses took Jethro's advice, delegating responsibility to judges and thus creating the basis for our modern court system. With a little less pressure on him, Moses went on to live to the ripe old age of 120. As the adage goes, delegate or disintegrate.

A piece of advice that I try to follow and that I frequently offer, often to the surprise of my students, is "Stop working so hard. Stop getting the most out of every single day." One student was confused; she was sure this sentence had a "typo" and was supposed to say, "Stop! Get the most out of every single day."

But not only is it impossible to get the most out of every day, trying to do so puts an unhealthy amount of pressure on us. My busy, high-achieving students often argue that it is an inherent Jewish cultural value to be an overachiever. As the joke goes, "When is a Jewish fetus considered viable? When it graduates from medical school." Achieving success in our lives *is* important, but I like to remind my students of the message we received on Sinai. "Remember the thunder and lightning, the trembling mountain? The big moment of awe?" I say. "What did God tell us that day on Mount Sinai? Take a day off every single week!"

The biblical book of Ecclesiastes also makes the point that we need to stop working so hard, and teaches us that we should look to nature for examples of how to properly balance our lives.

The author of Ecclesiastes, King Kohelet, was obsessed with the futility of life. Frankly, he probably could have used some serious antidepressants. As he pessimistically saw it, we can try, and try, and try to change the world, but nothing really changes or has a lasting impact. Despite his gloomy outlook, though, he does have some good advice for us, and his words, ironically, have endured and remain applicable thousands of years after his death.

King Kohelet wrote, "All streams flow into the sea, / Yet the sea is never full" (Ecclesiastes 1:7). Like the commandment that we observe the Sabbath, this verse offers a much needed antidote to our workaholic culture, which encourages our work lives to spill over and engulf every other aspect of our lives. The ancient voice of King Kohelet calls out to us through the centuries saying that all the rivers in the world work together day and night, 24/7, without pause, to try to fill the sea. And yet despite this 100 percent effort, they still can't do it. So why are you trying so hard to fill up your metaphorical seas? Are you so much more powerful, efficient, and capable than nature that you can do better than all the rivers? Why are you working so hard?

Even God didn't work 24/7. It was more like 24/6. You probably remember the story of Creation from the beginning of the Bible: God created the world in six days, and on the seventh day God rested. God managed to fit a day off into even this jam-packed week, during which He had to form all those planets and design the "wild beasts of every kind and cattle of every kind, and all kinds of creeping things of the earth" (Genesis 1:25). Talk about a busy week! And of course, this is why both Christianity and Judaism preach that six days a week we toil within the world—building, creating, and tending—but on the seventh day we should refrain from working. We model ourselves after God, and so like God we set aside the seventh day to enjoy what God created rather than continue creating ourselves. And, importantly, on the seventh day, a day without our work, we also see that the world can and will survive without us.

So how do we put some balance back into our lives? How do we nudge ourselves even a smidgen toward a healthy work-life balance? The key may be in the instruction that the seventh day is a time not to create, but rather to enjoy what God has created. What is God's Creation other than us? The rest of the natural world, of course.

Nature is a great teacher and role model for finding balance. Natural systems are continually seeking equilibrium and rebalancing themselves. It is obvious when natural systems are out of whack. When there is too much water, for example, it floods. If there is way too much water, then think Noah and the animals clomping two by two into the ark. On the other hand, when there is not enough water, we have a drought. Think Joseph's family going down to Egypt to buy grain from Pharaoh's storehouses. We know how that one worked out; it took us four hundred years to get home! We like to think that we can control the natural world and compensate for imbalances within the system. But out power is finite.

The way we treat the earth is the same way we treat our own bodies. When I don't get enough sleep, I go get a large, skinny *café au lait,* extra foam please, dash of chocolate on top. What do people do when they can't sleep because their minds are still racing at the end of a busy day? That's nothing a [fill in the name of your little pill of choice] can't fix.

Unfortunately, the preventive medicine of taking a day

off each week just doesn't seem to fit into our busy lives. But we cannot sustain these artificialities forever. Eventually, the entire system collapses. For years we have pumped carbon dioxide emissions into the air. The result? Climate change, which among other things has caused the sea temperatures to rise, causing intense storm cycles. And the result of that, according to some experts? The floods and hurricanes that have had a devastating impact on the country in the past few years.

So, too, without rest, our bodies break down. Carpal tunnel syndrome, heart disease, obesity, and strokes are just a few of the diseases that strike those who work too hard and without pause.

No system can be pushed relentlessly. Neither the air we breathe, nor the water we drink, nor our bodies, nor our souls. Every system needs a rest.

When we divorce ourselves from nature, we tend to forget about the cycles. We try to sustain a ceaseless, upward trajectory. It's easy to ignore the cycles of night and day, for example, when you can flip a switch and turn darkness into light and light into darkness. And too many of us ignore solutions as simple as this: I am tired. I think I will nap.

Although the Bible encourages us to fulfill our potential, it also teaches us to embrace the natural cycles that ebb and flow. Jewish tradition is deeply rooted in the natural cycles of the earth. One of my favorite rituals is the monthly celebration of the moon, which takes place when the moon is almost full. Traditionally, we bless the waxing moon while standing outside beneath the bright, white light of the moon. We say the appointed prayers and then rise up on our toes, as if lunging toward the sky. When I was young I was taught to jump toward the moon and say, "Just as the moon fulfills its potential of fullness, so too may I reach my potential."

What I love most about this ritual, though, besides that we can actually go outside, is what the moon does next. As soon as the moon gets full, it begins to wane again. The lesson is clear. Strive to reach your potential, but take time to rest. The moon cannot continually get larger; the idea that it could seems comical. It cannot wax constantly, nor can we.

Perhaps this need for "downtime" explains why God chose to include Sabbath rest as one of the Ten Commandments. Sabbath is one of the best tools we have for learning to rest and for recalibrating our lives to a more natural rhythm of work and rest. This is what the Bible says about the Sabbath:

> Remember the sabbath day and keep it holy. Six days you shall labor and do all your work, but the seventh day is a sabbath of the Lord your God: you shall not do any work—you, your son or daughter, your male or female slave, or your cattle, or the

stranger who is within your settlements. For in six days the Lord made heaven and earth and sea, and all that is in them, and He rested on the seventh day; therefore the Lord blessed the Sabbath day, and made it holy. (Exodus 20:8–11)

The directions given here for observing the Sabbath are rather simple and can be summarized as (1) Remember the Sabbath, (2) Keep it holy, and (3) Don't work! All that really nitpicky, specific stuff—like going to church or synagogue, not driving and not cooking—isn't actually in the Bible. People added those requirements later on.

How we are supposed to apply this commandment to our lives has been a source of debate for centuries, so now let's take a look at each part: "Remember the Sabbath," "Keep it holy," and "Don't work."

Remembering seems straightforward enough. If we choose to make something important enough, we won't forget it. One day out of seven shouldn't be too hard to keep track of on a calendar. My mother always marvels that the first thing I put into my calendar is my workout schedule, and then I schedule all my work appointments around that. "So that's how you make the time to train for triathlons, and write a book, and take care of a two-year-old!" she says. I do the same thing with the Sabbath, and you can too. Put that in first, then schedule around it. Okay, now that we are remembering the Sabbath, what are we going to do on the Sabbath?

This leads us to "Keep it holy" and "Don't work," the phrases that are sources of great confusion and consternation.

The Hebrew word for "holy," *kadosh*, literally means "set apart." The Sabbath day is set apart from all the other days of the week. It is different, and the difference is part of what makes it holy. This is reflected in practically everything we do, or are supposed to do, on the Sabbath. For example, Jewish people traditionally eat challah, a braided bread, on the Sabbath. Why braided? Because during the rest of the week our bread is not braided. Similarly, Jews tear the challah on the Sabbath, rather than cut it with a knife, because during the rest of the week we slice our bread with a knife. (Does that mean that challah was the best invention *before* sliced bread?) And of course the "biggie," on the Sabbath: we don't work, because during the rest of the week we do have to work.

The crux is, what does it mean to work? In Judaism, an ancient definition of work leads to restrictions on all sorts of things we love to do today, but which didn't even exist when the rule was written over two thousand years ago. For example, bike riding is out. Why? Although riding a bike is arguably permissible (as long as you don't exert yourself), you might accidentally ride over a nail and then have to fix a flat tire on your bike. That is not permitted, because traditionally fixing things is considered work. In the strictest application of Jewish law, the only exception to the ban on work on Sabbath is to save a life.

Many of the Sabbath activities that I consider opportunities for spiritual rejuvenation and communion with God others consider work. This is sometimes a source of tension between my orthodox colleagues and me. On Sabbath, my family and I choose to hike, ski, bike, and trail run. For me, these activities are restful, despite my friend's teasing, "Why run if no one is chasing you?" How do I reconcile my experience with tradition?

When the concept of Sabbath was first created, people lived very different lives than we do today. They toiled physically all week, carrying, pushing, heaving, lifting, cutting, sewing, and sweating. The Sabbath offered them a respite from their toil, a chance to sit quietly, to read, to study, to eat leisurely meals, and to visit with friends and family.

But today work looks very different from the way it did for our great-great-grandparents. For many of us, work means being inside an office, usually sitting at a desk staring at a computer screen, talking on the phone, or sitting in endless meetings. Getting outside on the Sabbath and digging a garden or strapping a pack on your back and hiking a ridge is often a welcome respite from the rest of the week's labors.

Sometimes, having time for strenuous physical activity

is also part of what sets Sabbath apart from the rest of the week.

Those of us who are not constrained by the strict interpretation of Jewish law need to answer the question of "What is work?" for ourselves. How do you make a day holy and set it apart from all the other days? What is spiritually nourishing and inspirational to you?

On Adventure Rabbi trips, for example, we celebrate the Sabbath by hiking through winding canyon trails, climbing to the tops of craggy peaks, and skiing untracked powder. We immerse ourselves in the natural world in our attempt to reconnect with ourselves, our community, and the Creator.

We move at a different pace than we do the rest of the week. And because we want to hike together as a community, we generally move more slowly and leisurely than we would as individuals. We pause, for example, to notice the colors of the clouds hovering over the ridgeline—not just a single monotone shade of gray, but subtle shades of yellow, pink, and purple, reflecting the soft morning light. We sit beneath the cliffs and listen as the cliff swallows swoop in and out of their nests, their calls reverberating deep into the earth.

I've led Sabbath services on a frozen lake that we snowshoed to, through snow so deep it was up to our thighs. And then, beneath a wide blue sky, we sang traditional Hebrew prayers and added thoughts of our own.

I've led Sabbath hikes to the top of hills overlooking the city. As we rested, contentedly warming ourselves on sun-baked granite slabs, we debated biblical concepts, using traditional texts, but adding our own modern sensibilities.

I teach that on the Sabbath, it is important to carefully choose what we speak about. I ask those who come to celebrate Sabbath with me to consciously try to leave out complaints about work, for example, so that we can begin to shed the stress of the workweek. Instead we must attempt to engross ourselves in the joy of being outdoors and celebrate the fourth commandment: rest.

At the end of my Sabbath outings, our bodies are frequently exhausted, but pleasantly so. Our backs may ache from heavy packs, and our leg muscles may be taut from an intense climb. But our hearts are joyful, our minds inspired, and our souls soar high above the ground on which we walk.

I passionately believe that each of us needs to figure out a way to remember the Sabbath, to keep it holy and to rest. For me, it means taking time to be with myself, my family, and my community, immersed in the miracle of God's Creation.

Although in Exodus 31:15 the Bible says, "Six days may work be done, but on the seventh day there shall be a sabbath of complete rest, holy to the Lord; whoever does work on the sabbath day shall be put to death," I do not believe anyone is going to get the death penalty for going grocery shopping, running errands, or checking e-mail on the Sabbath. But I do believe that if we do not take a day off each week to decompress and reconnect, we are slowly and steadily killing ourselves.

Thousands of years ago our ancestors stood at the base of Mount Sinai and received a wondrous gift—the Ten Commandments—which included a revolutionary charge: rest one day a week. Today we continue to unpack that gift as we struggle to understand what it means. The Sabbath is your inheritance. It is yours to claim, to safeguard, and to make meaningful in a way that works for you.

And now it is time for you to ask yourself: What does it mean to you? How will you remember the Sabbath day? How will you set it apart from the rest of the week, and how will you keep it holy?

Here are some ideas to start thinking about. Perhaps choose an appliance that you will not use for twenty-four hours, maybe the dishwasher or the washer and dryer. One of my adult bat mitzvah students, Rachael, doesn't use the microwave because the microwave is all about speed, and Sabbath is all about slowing down. Another of my students will write e-mails but doesn't send them out until after the Sabbath is over!

One of my students loves the idea of using reusable cloth bags at the grocery store, but he never manages to get that organized when he hurriedly picks up a few things after work during the week. But when he shops on the Sab-

bath, he always uses reusable cloth bags so that he consumes at least a bit less and gives the earth a day off too.

There are a myriad of ways to set the Sabbath apart, to
create opportunities to rediscover awe, to notice burning
bushes, and, most important, to rest. Remember, only you
can decide which is the correct path for you! Experiment
and see what works best. Be bold! If you don't like how
one Sabbath plan works out, try something else. Sabbath
should be a gift, not a burden.

If you are anything like me, at this point in the book
you're starting to wonder how you can possibly fit all this
into your life. The "to-do" list keeps getting longer: create
a meaningful, restful Sabbath; rediscover awe; take the ini-
tiative; open your eyes. If you are beginning to feel that
way, don't panic. Great news lies ahead; even Moses was
not perfect—and neither, I'll argue, is God.

# CHAPTER 5

# Stop Trying So Hard!
# Even God Isn't Perfect

*And God said to Moses, "I am who I am."*

—Exodus 3:14

I know we all say that nobody is perfect, but I'm not quite sure that I believe it. I haven't let go of my fantasy that there is a very exclusive club of perfect people. When I finally get it right, I will get an e-mail from them, in which they will congratulate me for a job well done and invite me to attend their superstealth, secret meetings for the perfectly perfect. This will be my indication that I have achieved perfection, and henceforth I will live my flawless life without second-guessing myself or making a mistake.

Part of why I insist on clinging to the possibility of achieving perfection is that our culture thrives on the pursuit of perfection. It almost feels like my patriotic duty to whiten my teeth and reduce my waistline. The quest to banish flaws from our lives drives our economy.

As a nation, we spend billions of dollars a year on our quests for perfect bodies. We join gyms, Bo-Tox our wrinkles, and highlight our hair. Yet despite all our efforts and dollars, few of us will ever compare to the ideals we hold.

And how much do we spend a year in pursuit of perfect lawns—spraying fertilizer, laying down sod, or hiring a gardener—and yet the grass is still greener on the other side.

Our culture's pursuit of perfection is one of the major stumbling blocks between us and contentment. We divorce our mates, fire our rabbis or ministers, and change our children's schools, all in search of something better, which we are sure is right around the corner. Yet somehow it never is. Each new situation brings its own disappointments.

It's almost as if we believe that we are entitled to perfect lives. If we could just get it right, then perfect jobs, perfect homes, and perfect partners would be within our reach.

How did we come to even think that perfection was a possible goal? Perhaps it began with our ability to have dominion over the earth. We can stop imperfect forest fires with chemical fire retardants, fight imperfect infections with antibiotics, cool the imperfect summer heat with air-conditioning, and kill off imperfect mosquitoes with DDT.

We have established control over imperfect nature. So why not perfect everything?

Ironically, as we have become masters of our environments and walled ourselves off from nature, we have lost sight of the beauty of Creation's idiosyncrasies and the importance of its imperfections. This tree is beautiful because the scaled texture of its bark is different from that one's. This river is beautiful because it curves and bends differently from that one.

We have forgotten the ways in which each creature fits into the balance of the larger ecosystem. For example, years of suppressing wildfires ultimately results in more fuel for massive fires, which burn homes and wildlife habitat.

Is our improved version of the world really so much better than God's original Creation? Is a rose garden, each petal carefully bred for magnificent color and shape, more breathtaking than the cacophony of colors in a wildflower meadow? Is a river straightened by the Army Corps of Engineers an improvement? The concrete riverbanks that line many city rivers control erosion, but they also take away the wetlands where frogs and fish thrive. It's not always clear-cut which is better.

Part of nature's beauty is its imperfection. Seldom does an evergreen have the perfect shape of a picture-book Christmas tree. Yet is it not still beautiful?

Those who spend a lot of time outdoors tend to relish

nature's imperfection. We fight to preserve nature rather than to improve it. Perhaps the only perfect thing about nature is its acceptance of imperfection.

Not surprisingly, I was up in the mountains immersed in nature when I finally got it that perfection is not achievable. I remember the exact day I realized nobody was perfect. It was late summer and I was mountain biking with my friend Beth, who to this day is one of the strongest athletes I have ever met. Summer was coming to a close, and I was reluctantly getting ready to leave Colorado to return to the seminary in Cincinnati. Beth was about seven minutes ahead of me on the trail, as she always was. Despite a summer of chasing her up mountains on my mountain bike, I still could not keep up! As I climbed, I wished that my friends at school could be more like Beth—easygoing, yet tenacious and disciplined when it came to her sports.

Inevitably, as happens when we start to compare people, soon I was thinking about all the qualities Beth was working on. She would be the first to admit that she is not perfect. And that is when my worldview began to unravel. I went through the list of all my friends: no perfect people. My family: no perfect people. My professors: no perfect people. Then I jumped to the Bible and the other holy texts. No perfect people. I was stunned. I felt like I had been thrown over the handlebars of my bike and landed in a heap on the ground. Nobody is perfect!

I looked around at the bristlecone pines, which appeared stunted and twisted, bent by relentless wind and storms. Yet the eerie-looking tree is perfectly adapted for the harsh alpine conditions of wind and snow and is known for its longevity. At the same time I thought about the biblical characters such as Isaac, Rebecca, and Jacob, each admirable in some ways and despicable in others, but certainly far from perfect, and that's when I finally put it all together.

Religion, like nature, does not ask us to be perfect. Rather, nature and religion offer to teach us about the spirituality of imperfection.

The Bible does not even set up perfection as a goal for us to achieve. The Bible does give us a day called Yom Kippur, translated as the "Day of Atonement," which focuses on imperfection. But perfection is not the goal. The Bible says, "On the tenth day of this seventh month there shall be a day of atonement" (Leviticus 23:27). The text continues, "You shall do no manner of work: it shall be a statute for ever throughout your generations in all your dwellings" (Leviticus 23:31). (JB)

The Day of Atonement is part of the holiest time of the Jewish year. Each year Jews devote the entire month preceding the Day of Atonement to contemplating our behavior during the past year. Where have we fallen short? When were we not our best selves?

Jewish people collectively set aside this time to learn about ourselves and take responsibility for our actions. We are supposed to apologize directly to those we have hurt and then make compensation for the harm we have inflicted. Most important, we are to work to change our ways so that given the same situation, we will not repeat the same mistake. Finally, on Yom Kippur we gather as a community to atone.

What I find most inspirational about this holiday is what we don't say. There is no prayer asking, "Oh Lord our God, may this be the year that we get it right. In the year to come, may we make no mistakes so that next year we have no need for repentance or Yom Kippur." There is no expectation that we should be perfect and therefore no prayer asking that we will not need time for apologizing on Yom Kippur. Perfection is not the goal or the expectation.

Some religious people adamantly disagree and argue that everything in the world is perfect. We've all heard the argument that God is perfect, and since God is in everything, then everything must be perfect. According to this line of reasoning, the imperfections of life—its difficulties and challenges—are meant to help us learn and improve. God only gives us what we need, and what we can handle. Pain and suffering are part of a larger picture, one that we can't quite understand. We must trust that everything happens for a reason and is for the best. Ultimately, everything is unfolding according to God's perfect plan.

I don't think so. You and I are both imperfect and so is our world. Therefore bad things happen, even to good people, and it's a really big bummer when they do. Bad things don't happen for a preordained reason. They just happen. Now let's start dealing with it.

Quite in contrast to being perfect or even mandating that we strive for perfection, what God and religion do is give us great role models for accepting our imperfections and working with what we have. Think about it—is anyone in the Bible without flaw?

Even Moses (as in the Five Books of Moses) is imperfect. Moses had a stutter, or some sort of speech impediment. Today he would have been sent to a speech pathologist. But instead God sends him to speak to Pharaoh, the most powerful ruler in the land! When God tells him to go to Pharaoh, Moses protests and pleads not to go, saying, "I am slow of speech and slow of tongue" (Exodus 4:10).

Adding imperfection to imperfection, Moses was a reluctant leader. When God asks him to be God's spokesperson to Pharaoh, rather than eagerly accepting the assignment, Moses implores God to pick a better-qualified person. He questions whether God is making the right choice, and it never occurs to him that God can prepare him for the task. Moses has a serious confidence problem. Not only does he doubt himself, but he doubts God. Moses says to God, "But, behold they will not believe me, nor listen to my voice; for they will say, The Lord has not appeared to you" (Exodus 4:1).

Even once Moses becomes the leader, he often can't

quite figure out what is required of him and doubts his own ability. He continually needs to go back to God for more instruction. Remember the Red Sea story? It's Nachshon who jumps into the water, not Moses.

And what's more, Moses' temper was famous. He calls his followers "rebels," and he gets frustrated with the officers of the army. Because of one particularly volatile and angry outburst, God decides not to allow Moses to enter the Promised Land. You might remember the incident—it is when Moses hits a rock with his staff instead of asking it to spew forth water for the thirsty Israelites. What makes the incident so terrible is that Moses makes it seem like he and Aaron are producing the water, using some sort of magic, rather than making it clear that God is providing the water. That is a big whoops. As a result, in a heart-wrenching scene, God tells Moses he will not be allowed to enter the Promised Land: " 'This is the land of which I swore to Abraham, Isaac, and Jacob, "I will assign it to your offspring." I have let you see it with your own eyes, but you shall not cross there.' So Moses the servant of the Lord died there, in the land of Moab, at the command of the Lord" (Deuteronomy 34:4–5).

Moses may have been the greatest prophet ever, as the Bible says. Moses may have met God face-to-face. But he was not perfect. He had a stutter, was reluctant to answer God's call to lead, had a heated temper, repeatedly doubted God, and was paralyzed by his own self-doubt.

Surely there must have been a better person for the job! We can only assume that Moses' imperfection is part of what makes him such a great leader and a role model for us.

Despite Moses' limitations, God chose Moses. And despite his imperfection, Moses got the job done. He led the people out of the house of bondage, secured the Ten Commandments, talked God out of destroying the Israelites, and, ultimately, he led them through the wilderness to the edge of the Promised Land.

Never, through all of their years together, did God ask Moses to be perfect or to be anything other than who he was. God never tried to "perfect" Moses.

You see, when it comes to creating perfect people, God is in a bind. God could have made Moses (and all the rest of us) perfect. If humanity was 100 percent good, all of the world's troubles would be over. But God wants us to have free will, to be able to choose good over evil. So, for example, God waited to see if Moses would turn aside to notice the burning bush, and then God spoke to him. God waited to see if Nachshon would step into the river, and then God parted the sea.

If we don't have a choice of how to behave, then we are only being good because we have to be. We become like the angels in heaven, who by design are able only to heed God's will, never veering to the left or the right. If that were how we lived on earth, life would be predictable and dull, and there would never be lessons to learn, or qualities to improve upon. How much more fulfilling life is when we must *choose* the right path! So what is God to do? God made us imperfect and modeled for us the path to righteousness.

I believe that it is wrong to say that everything is perfect including God; on the contrary, nothing is perfect. Not even God. The God portrayed in the Bible makes tons of mistakes and doesn't seem to get all that worked up about it. Since we were created in God's image, we can look to God as a role model for how to live as imperfect beings. We can let God's mistakes serve as a "how-to guide" for us to deal with our own inherent flaws and the flaws of our world. In this way, God's modeling of imperfection can liberate us from our ever-frustrated expectations of perfection.

God's mistakes start right in the beginning of the Bible. Everything is going along well until on the sixth day of Creation God created man and woman. Oddly, it is not clear exactly how God felt about the finished product. After creating each of the other creatures—fish, birds, creepy crawly things, wild beasts, and cattle—the text says, "and God saw that this was good." But after God created mankind the text is silent, as if God was still deciding whether creating humanity was a good move or not.

A few passages later in the Bible, after several generations come and go, God realizes that making mankind was a mistake. God discovers that humanity has a propensity toward wickedness, and now God regrets the decision to create man. The text tells us, "And the Lord regretted that He had made man on earth, and His heart was saddened" (Genesis 6:6).

God is not all knowing, at least not at this point, because God didn't know how making mankind was going to work out. And clearly it didn't work out as God had planned. What does God model for us? When you make a mistake, try to fix it.

God decides to destroy mankind, and most of Creation, since man had corrupted the rest of the world, and start over with Noah, his family, and a group of carefully selected animals. "The Lord said, 'I will blot out from the earth the men whom I created—men together with beasts, creeping things, and birds of the sky; for I regret that I made them' " (Genesis 6:7).

God creates a flood of draconian proportions. Men, women, and children die in the rising waters, drowned along with countless numbers of animals of all sizes, shapes, and colors. "All existence on the earth was blotted out—man, cattle, creeping things, and birds of the sky; they were blotted out from the earth. Only Noah was left, and those with him in the ark" (Genesis 7:23).

Now at last the world would be perfect. Evil would be banished from the earth. But the last animal has barely left the ark, and the water on the ground is not yet dry, when God realizes that the flood is not going to work. Destroying all life is not going to change humanity. God realizes there is something inherent in humans that makes us pursue that which is evil. Causing the flood was a mistake. God says, "Never again will I doom the earth because of man, since the devisings of man's mind are evil from his youth; nor will I ever again destroy every living being, as I have done" (Genesis 8:21).

This is God's next lesson for us about imperfection. If you try to fix your mistake and it doesn't work, don't keep doing the same thing. Learn from your mistakes, apologize, and then try something different. There are lots of solutions out there. Keep on trying! That is what God does.

God makes a covenant with Noah in which God promises never again to destroy the world by flood. The rainbow, the Bible says, is the sign for all time that God remembers His promise. In the same covenant, God allows humans to eat meat, in addition to the vegetation they were given for food in the Creation story. Some rabbis teach that God hoped that killing and eating animals would channel human aggression, and slaughtering animals would dissipate the urge to kill other humans. To this end, God says, "Every creature that lives shall be yours to eat; as with the green grasses, I give you all these" (Genesis 9:3).

As we know, these guidelines didn't work either. I

guess there is only so much good a rainbow and a burger can do. By chapter 19 of Genesis, the story of the infamous cities of Sodom and Gomorrah, the people were so thoroughly wicked that God was unable to find even ten righteous people in either city. So God sends the few righteous people off to a safe location and then kills off the rest of the inhabitants, also wiping out the grasses, gardens, and trees. I guess they had been corrupted too. The text reads, "[God] annihilated those cities and the entire Plain, and all the inhabitants of the cities and the vegetation of the ground" (Genesis 19:25).

Despite the fact that God has not yet figured out how to fix the world or us, God does not give up. God keeps on trying to make things better. God gave us the Bible to live by, hoping the commandments would straighten us out. When that didn't work, God sent us prophets to guide us and implore us to change. When we failed to listen to them, God sent us sages and scholars to teach us and guide us. And in case that didn't work, God gave us texts explaining ways to find consolation and comfort as we struggle to deal with the imperfections of ourselves and the world. We will look at some of these sources of comfort in chapter 7, "Restore Your Soul Beside Still Waters."

The teaching is this: Life is not perfect. Rather life is filled with wrenching imperfection. Our task is neither to try to be perfect nor to demand perfection from others.

I'm not suggesting that we shouldn't try to improve ourselves, or the world. We certainly should. But sometimes we try too hard and do more harm than good, as we will see in the next chapter. We forget that we are inherently imperfect and therefore must learn to be gentle with our own flaws and those of others. We must learn to cut ourselves some slack. We must be forgiving of our families, our friends, and our communities when they fall short of our expectations.

This is a difficult lesson to learn, and it goes contrary to most of what our society teaches. But only by accepting imperfection will we find the peace, tranquility, and comfort for which we all yearn.

Here is one of the practices I find helpful to work toward accepting my imperfection and that of others. It is very simplistic, but it is lovely in its ability to remind me that imperfection is part of nature and religion. I sit with my back against a tree (preferably an oddly shaped one) and concentrate on my breath. As I slowly breathe in and out, I bring my attention to the sensation of the tree trunk against my back and of the solid earth beneath me, holding me without judgment. Once I have slowed down enough to be fully present, I slowly repeat, again and again, the words God used to describe Himself to Moses: "I am who I am" (Exodus 3:13). Not "I am today who I am, but tomorrow I will be better." Just "I am who I am."

God does not ask us to be perfect. Religion does not ask us to be perfect. Nature does not ask us to be perfect. And even though our society often sets perfection as a goal, we must stop asking ourselves to be perfect.

You are an imperfect creature. So am I. So is the whole world. And that is absolutely perfect.

# Hear the Still, Small Voice Within

*And lo, the Lord passed by. There was a great
and mighty wind, splitting mountains and
shattering rocks by the power of the Lord; but
the Lord was not in the wind. After the wind—
an earthquake; but the Lord was not in the
earthquake. After the earthquake—fire; but the
Lord was not in the fire. And after the fire—
a still, small voice.*

—1 Kings 19:11–12

I buried another kayaker today. Actually, I can't say I buried him. They couldn't find the body. The search and rescue team says that when the spring runoff goes down, the river may give up the body. I officiated at the memorial service.

Three weeks earlier, the kayaker's twenty-nine-year-old friend—they had been teammates on their college ski team—had skied into a crevasse in France and died. The man skiing with him tried to save him, but also fell into the crevasse and perished. Now both of their bodies are buried deep within the glacier.

There seem to be more and more deaths like this lately. Not mediocre athletes who are in over their heads, although I've seen plenty of those, but athletes at the top of their game. The kayaker was one of the best paddlers in Colorado, if not the country. He had successfully run far more difficult rapids than the one that killed him. But that day, in the river in southern Colorado, the kayaker put in his paddle just a hair too early, or perhaps just a bit too late, and the mistake cost him his life.

In milliseconds, he was sucked into a hole and trapped in an underwater cave. Another boater went in after him to try to rescue him. The second kayaker reached out frantically, groping in the water to grab anything he could reach and, against all odds, was able to grasp his friend's hand for a moment, but then lost him once again to the unconquerable pull of the whirling waters. The kayaker was last seen as he washed down the rapids and disappeared over a waterfall into the deep, churning waters below.

When his father called me, the search was on day three. "How long do they look before they presume he is dead?" I naïvely asked. He answered, "Oh, all the boaters know that on this mile stretch of class-five rapids, if you don't make it through, you die." He paused before continuing, "We know he is dead. We're just hoping to have a body to bury."

I'm seeing more and more tragedies like this, athletes pushing the envelope as they try to find their limits on bigger water, longer runs, or higher mountains. People searching for the perfect run, the perfect route, or the perfect climb. Sometimes, most of the time, they make it back and get to tell and retell the details of their adventures. Other times they find their limit. When we are lucky, we find their bodies. If not, we hope the river will give them up when the spring runoff goes down.

The kayaker's friends were shocked by his death. They said things like: "It couldn't happen to him." And "He backed off from runs when it didn't feel right." And "He was the best, not particularly foolhardy." But his mother and grandmother were not surprised. They had been waiting for years for the phone call, which finally came from one of the kayaker's friends. "We were running a stretch of river down south by Durango. It had been the perfect run. And then something went wrong. He never came out of the canyon. We promise we will keep looking until we find him."

The more I learned about the kayaker, the less I, like his mother or grandmother, was surprised about his death. The kayaker spent his life pushing limits, and he was going to keep on pushing until something pushed back.

His family shared his photo album with me, and what I found amazing was what they considered normal. For example, when they showed me pictures of the kayaker and his friends backcountry skiing, his father said, "See that avalanche chute? It's about to slide. Here they are in the next picture as it releases, ten feet away from where they're standing. And here they are in the next picture skiing down after it."

Now, I've done my share of backcountry skiing, and my husband worked as ski patroller at a Colorado resort where his job, for several years, was to use high explosives to intentionally trigger avalanches in order to make the terrain safe for skiers. One thing I have learned about avalanches is this: if you are only ten feet away from a slide when it releases in the backcountry, you are way too close.

The kayaker's sister told me stories of the nights the kayaker and his friends spent in snow caves. It was a circumstance that seemed to be repeated every winter. She said, "They were skiing to a backcountry hut when a blizzard hit and they were unable to ski any farther. They dug a snow cave and spent the night." His family remarked how chivalrous he had been, giving all the food and water to the women, since there was not enough for everyone. The stories went on and on, all extreme situations that have come to be considered "normal." Acceptable risk.

This world is familiar to me. For years I ran ultramarathons in which it was unfortunate, but not terribly uncommon, for runners to end up on kidney dialysis after a race. The prophylactic drugs we overused on a regular basis, such as ibuprofen and naproxen, combined with intense exertion and not enough water, can shut down a runner's kidneys. That was part of the deal. "Normal." Acceptable risk.

I ran a hundred-mile ultramarathon called the Leadville Trail 100. As the highest ultramarathon race in the world its motto is No Limits. When the race director proposed the creation of the now annual event, everyone told him he was crazy. They said that the mixture of high altitude, mountainous terrain, and one-hundred-mile distance would literally kill all the race entrants.

No Limits became my motto, too. Ninety-four miles into the one-hundred-mile race, after I had been running continuously for twenty-seven and a half hours, I could hardly breathe. I was running at an elevation well over ten thousand feet and my lungs were filling with fluid. The condition is called pulmonary edema and can happen to even the most fit, acclimatized athletes. I remember very clearly thinking, "If I collapse here and stop breathing, it will only take someone two minutes to get to the road if they cut through those trees. Help could be here in four minutes and I wouldn't be brain dead until six minutes." I remember that seemed okay with me. Acceptable risk.

(I managed to make it the last six miles and not collapse until the finish line, where thanks to modern medicine's miracle drugs, the hospital staff had me breathing normally within twenty-four hours. I never did actually stop breathing.)

In many ways, my warped state of mind was similar to that of a kayaker boating down a stretch of river where if you make a single mistake you die.

How did this come to be normal? Why do I and people like me feel the need to push the limits to such abnormal extremes?

Our culture, especially for those of us who live out west, is all about breaking limits. We don't want any limits imposed on us. We want to discover the limits ourselves. The motto No Limits has become the motto of our time.

In contrast, religion is all about limits and boundaries. Eat this, don't eat that. Marry this person, not that person. This day is holy, this day is mundane. Do this, don't do that. Maybe that is part of why religion is unpopular with certain segments of our population. Could it be that rejecting religion is about rejecting limits? Saying, "Don't tell me what I can and cannot do."

Limits, we like to think, are a thing of the past. Our parents and grandparents had limits. In "those" days women were limited in their job choices. Jews and people of color couldn't join certain country clubs, work in certain hospitals or at exclusive firms. One of the major hospitals in

Denver, Colorado, was founded by Jewish doctors because the other hospitals wouldn't hire Jewish doctors. So they started their own.

Today we like to teach that there are no limits to what you can be, where you can live, what you can earn, or what you can accomplish. If we just push hard enough, we can achieve those perfect lives. I find that in the outdoor, athletic world there are far fewer limits than there were even ten years ago. Lighter, stronger, and more precise gear, coupled with expanded transportation opportunities, enable us to go places no one has gone before. The world is our playground.

But are there side effects of our limitless lifestyle? Yes, and that is what the kayaker discovered on that devastating day in the canyon.

Two weeks after the kayaker died, I was called upon to officiate at another funeral. In some ways the two deaths couldn't have been more different. In other ways they were eerily the same. The second funeral was for a prominent infectious disease doctor, who died of cancer at the age of sixty-four. The doctor lived just about twice as long as the kayaker and, unlike the kayaker, who was at the beginning of his career, the doctor had had a profoundly successful career, in which he saved thousands of lives. Perhaps more important, he shared his knowledge and skills with countless physicians, nurse practitioners, and other medical specialists.

The similarity was that the doctor, like the kayaker, was a limit pusher. He pushed the limits of diagnosis and treatment and as a result he saved countless lives.

Not surprisingly, he also pushed the limits of work-life balance. His passion for medicine, his talent for figuring out the key to puzzling illness, led him to work fourteen to twenty hours a day, seven days a week. He never took a vacation. He rarely was home for dinner with his family. A concept like Sabbath rest with family was something he read about in books but never actually had time for.

After a full day of work, empathizing with patients and supporting colleagues, the doctor found he had nothing left for his family. When he finally came home at the end of the day, he was so worn out that he was unable to be emotionally intimate with his wife and children. Rather, he would sit and read journals, rehash cases, or write articles and books. Some patients and colleagues said he was the perfect doctor because he was so devoted to his work.

Ultimately, his wife and children learned that they had to go on with their lives without him. The doctor moved south to pursue his upwardly spiraling career, and his family stayed in their hometown and continued to pursue the other, less glamorous parts of life like homework, soccer practice, and vacations. The family separated geographically and spiritually for many, many years. The doctor had sacrificed his relationship with his family for his career.

At the age of sixty-two, the doctor was diagnosed with

cancer. Faced with the reality that the time he had always waited for—"just let me finish this one diagnosis and then I'll be home"—was never going to arrive, he finally turned back to his wife and children. During the final two years of his life, he and his wife lived in the same town and had two years together to try to heal the wounds of his many years of absence. He connected with his now adult son and daughter and tried as best he could to make up for decades of lost time.

He became the loving, attentive, and emotive spouse and father that he was never able to be when he was well. He promised that if he beat his cancer, he would go on a vacation with his family. Sadly, he died in June 2006. The greater medical community, literally spread around the world, mourned the loss of this successful, talented, and compassionate soul. Yet the brilliant doctor, having rediscovered the unparalleled joy of being a husband and father, died with searing regret. He was so deeply saddened by the choices he had made.

After he died, I sat in his living room with a few members of his family and scores of his colleagues. There was such a disturbing dissonance between the doctor that his colleagues knew—after all, they had spent so much time with him—and the man his family knew. For example, his mother didn't even know about the magic tricks he did, bringing cheer to patients and colleagues alike. In the medical world, they were his "trademark"—simple, uplifting tricks that brought brief moments of joy into rooms other-wise filled with despair. How wrong it felt that his work life was so much more important than his home life, so that his colleagues knew him far better than his own family!

Before the doctor died, he was very specific about what he wanted said at his funeral. Looking back at his life and his brilliant career, he asked that I share this advice with his colleagues: "Tell them not to do it. Tell them it isn't worth it. Tell them to make sure they have time for their families and not to be seduced by the prestige, fulfill-ments, and joy of work. In the end, it is not enough. Tell them to go home."

The doctor, like the kayaker, pushed the limits. One pushed the limits of physical ability. The other, the limits of work-life balance. Ultimately, the kayaker killed himself. The doctor destroyed his family.

The heaviness of these few weeks has left me with questions. Why do we push so hard? What are we search-ing for? Is there anything that religion can offer us so that we can stop?

I searched for something in the Bible to help me wrap my head around this and was drawn to a powerful passage in First Kings. The story is about the prophet Elijah. Elijah is one of our most famous prophets. Even many people who are only peripherally in touch with religion have heard of Elijah, from a variety of symbols and songs. Eli-jah's polished silver goblet is prominently displayed on the

Jewish Passover Seder dinner table. And a highlight of the Seder for children is opening the door and inviting Elijah to come in for dinner. During Havdalah, the ritual with which Jews close the Sabbath, there is a lovely song about Eliyahu Ha-navi, Elijah the prophet.

The reason that Elijah has such a prominent role in Judaism is that it is his responsibility to assess when the world is ready for the messiah to come. Elijah travels the earth, often disguised as a disabled beggar or homeless person, and evaluates how we treat him. But, when the day arrives that Elijah is greeted by a world filled with kind, loving, generous people, Elijah will send back the report to God that we are ready for the messiah. I can't help but think about that when I see a panhandler on the street.

Before Elijah took on this job, he worked as a prophet. We read about him in the biblical books of First and Second Kings. Elijah was a very skilled and talented prophet. He prophesies on a big scale and often with a large dose of dramatic flare. He calls fire down from heaven to consume his enemies. He makes a widow's last handful of flour and the contents of her almost empty jug of oil last an abnormally long time. In one of the most moving scenes, Elijah brings a dead boy back to life. All of these acts are, of course, done with the power of God. Elijah acts as God's representative.

Because Elijah was God's prophet, God, by definition, was present in all the work Elijah did. Yet, when this great prophet looked to meet God for himself, listen to what happens. Even if you have never heard this story, I think you will find parts of it familiar.

Elijah walks into the wilderness for forty days and forty nights, until he comes to the mountain of God, Mount Horeb. Mount Horeb is located in the same part of the wilderness in which the burning bush story took place. We hear similar themes of needing to get out into the wilderness, to leave behind the tumult of civilization, in order to meet God. Perhaps even Elijah needs time to decompress from the unrelenting pressure of his life as a prophet, before he is ready to face God.

When Elijah reaches the mountain, God calls out to him, "Why are you here, Elijah?" (1 Kings 19:9), as if to say, "What are you looking for? What is it that you seek?" The text continues with this incredible description of Elijah meeting the Creator:

> And lo, the Lord passed by. There was a great and mighty wind, splitting mountains and shattering rocks by the power of the Lord; but the Lord was not in the wind. After the wind—an earthquake; but the Lord was not in the earthquake. After the earthquake—fire; but the Lord was not in the fire. And after the fire—a still, small voice. (1 Kings 19:11–12)

God was not in the big, dramatic moments of the wind, the earthquake, or the fire, but in the quiet moment that followed. God was in the still, small voice. The lesson for us is this: We, like the kayaker and the doctor, tend to look for meaning in the dramatic, big moments of life—wind, earthquakes, harder rapids, more patients, tougher cases, steeper mountains, exotic and hard-to-reach vacation spots, more prominence and prestige, spiraling acquisitions, and so on. One of my students calls these "Moses moments," like the ones we explored earlier—the burning bush, the splitting of the Red Sea, and the trembling mountain with its top all aflame.

But, despite Moses' experiences of God, which tended toward the dramatic, the object of *our* quest for meaning is discovered, like Elijah's, in the still, small voice. It's in the quiet moments of life, the ones we often rush through on our way to the bigger and better things. Finding fulfillment and contentment in life involves going deeper into the present moment, rather than rushing on to a bigger moment. It's about being fully present in the "here and now," whatever you are doing.

One of the better-known Jewish prayers is called the V'ahavtah. It is one of the prayers found in the mezuzah, a small box that hangs on the doorways of Jewish homes. People often mistake this object for a good luck charm or talisman, but it's not. The mezuzah is simply a container

for this very important prayer. It is placed on the doorways of our homes so that we will think about the words
that are inside it every time we walk by them. The prayer
contains these words from the biblical book of Deuteronomy:

> You shall love the Lord your God with all your
> heart and with all your soul and with all your
> might. Take to heart these instructions with which
> I charge you this day. Impress them upon your
> children. Recite them when you stay at home and
> when you are away, when you lie down and when
> you get up. (Deuteronomy 6:5–7)

The message of this biblical verse is that we should
seek out meaning in the everyday tasks of life. Don't seg-
regate spirituality to certain places or specific activities,
thus excluding it from the trivial, picking-up-your-dirty-
socks tasks of life. When you sit in your house, go about
your business in the world, when you go to sleep and when
you wake up, all the time, every moment is a perfect moment to open the door to spiritual connection.

There is a lovely Hasidic teaching that says, "Soon after
the death of Rabbi Moshe, Rabbi Mendel of Kotzk asked
one of his disciples: 'What was most important to your
teacher?'

"The disciple thought and then replied: 'Whatever he happened to be doing at the moment.' "*

The still, small voice is heard in "whatever we happen to be doing at the moment." We need to relearn how to hear that voice. Perhaps then we will no longer need to paddle our actual or metaphorical big waters. Where do we search for the still, small voice? In the quiet crevices of life. Here is what some of the participants on a recent Adventure Rabbi hike suggested: Watching raindrops slide down the windowsill. Drinking hot chocolate in front of the fire. Figuring out how to make my grandmother's chicken soup and making it for a friend. Writing a piece of poetry. Meeting friends at a coffeehouse before work. Lighting Sabbath candles. Anything I do for myself. Listening to loons on a lake in Maine. Really listening to my grandfather tell a story, even if I've heard it many times before. Walking on a trail in my neighborhood park.

When we are truly content with who we are in the world, we will not succumb to the seductive powers of accolades and spotlights. We will be able to run five miles and feel good about it, rather than needing to run twenty or fifty miles to feel good. We will be able to work fewer hours, even if it means less prestige and money. We will focus on being significant rather than being successful. We

*Martin Buber, *Tales of the Hasidim,* Book Two, The Later Masters (New York: Schocken Books, 1975), p. 173.

will be able to train and work at a level that is sustainable, a rate that continually builds us up rather than eventually breaks us down. We will feel able to take a day of rest once a week to connect with friends, family, self, and God, without feeling that we are falling behind.

I'm not saying we should give up our careers or outdoor passions. I know all too well that after a day of staring at my computer screen I am not ready to go to yoga class, let alone sit still on a cushion and meditate. Call me a junkie, but I still need to grab my running shoes and run for an hour on the mountain trails behind our home. I need to move, and push, and be alone in the mountains where my soul thrives.

But I do recognize that on the path to peace I need to push a bit less and respect limits a bit more. I need to challenge myself to spend less time climbing the high peaks and more time sitting still and listening. I need to rush less from place to place, and go deeper into the place I am. Somewhere there is a middle ground, and our task is to find it.

I'll close with this story. When I brought my two-year-old daughter to school one morning, her classmate (he is in the full-day program) announced happily, "Sadie's home!"

His enthusiastic welcome warmed my heart. I am so glad that we had found a school environment where the children feel like they are family and Sadie can be well cared for in the mornings while I write. But, at the same time, it saddened me that this two-year-old boy spends so much time at school that he confuses it with home.

The time has come for us to say "No!" to the lures of grandeur that take us away from the core of our lives and the sounds of our souls. The time has come for us to quiet our lives and mute the distractions of our overstimulated society. The time has come for us to return to Elijah's wilderness, to hear and see the quiet truths that await us there. The time has come for us to turn inward, to our inner circles, and our inner voices. God is not in the wind, the earthquake, or the fire. God is in the still, small voice. The time has come for us to listen.

# CHAPTER 7

# Restore Your Soul
# Beside Still Waters

*The Lord is my Shepherd I shall not want.*
*He makes me to lie down in green pastures;*
*he leads me beside the still waters.*

—Psalm 23:1–2 (JB)

For millennia, humans and animals alike have congregated at watering holes. Although most of us no longer need to go to the stream or well to quench our physical thirst, I believe we still unconsciously seek out water to satisfy our spiritual thirst.

Why water? We all know intuitively that there is something comforting about bodies of water. When we face the imperfections of our world, when we feel sad or lonely, many of us go down to the lake to skip rocks, or to just sit and think. For example, during the heavy grief that filled our community after the consecutive deaths of the kayaker and then the doctor, I often rode my bike out to one of our smaller ponds, sat with my back against a cottonwood tree, dangled my feet in the cool water, and felt comforted.

Perhaps we are drawn to water because deep within our psyche lies an ancient yearning, an awareness of an innate connection to water. Our biblical ancestors were in touch with this and considered water to be spiritually restorative and soothing. Consider Psalm 23, a psalm frequently read at funerals:

> *The Lord is my Shepherd*
> *I shall not want.*
> *He makes me to lie down in green pastures;*
> *he leads me beside the still waters.*

> (Psalm 23:1–2)

For centuries, this Psalm's poignant message has provided comfort to Jews and Christians alike. Some people think of this Psalm as a Christian text, but it is from the original Jewish Bible and is part of our shared heritage.

The Psalmist (the writer of the Psalm) reflects on ways in which God shepherds us, guiding us through times of sadness and grief. God is the comfort and hope that leads us "through the valley of the shadow of death," back into the light of life.

But how does God console us? This, not surprisingly, is

the crux of the lesson, and the reason Psalm 23 is in my book about outdoor spiritual portals. The Psalm does not say, "God leads me to church or synagogue to sit and recite prayers." Nor does it say, "God urges me to open my Bible to Psalms of hope." No, Psalm 23 says, "God leads me beside the still waters."

The ancient wisdom of this message is very clear: "Go outside!" Experience God's presence through God's Creation—nature. This is why I find it terribly troublesome that modern religion skips over this powerful passage and views it as mere metaphor. Even those of us who are not "outdoors people" know that water, still or moving, and nature in general can be incredibly comforting. When we sit and read about "still water" and "green pastures" in the seats of a sanctuary but do not move on to experience them, are we missing out on a very important spiritual opportunity?

Water—walking by a lake as the sun rises, or even soaking in a hot bath at the end of a day—comforts us. Is it the primal connection to the soothing waters of the womb? Is it a psychic return to primordial waters from which all life arose, reconnecting us with all life on earth?

Even my daughter, Sadie, who is still too young to read biblical text, experiences the soothing power of water. When Sadie was almost one, my husband and I took her to California for a wedding. Between the crowded flight, the changes in altitude, our odd schedule, and the unfamiliar surroundings, Sadie was a wreck. Despite my husband's and my efforts to comfort her, her small sobs soon turned into torrents of weeping and screaming. After trying everything we could to console her, we took her down to the beach.

Soon we were surrounded by the sound of waves crashing on the sand and rolling softly back into the sea. The whistle of sandpipers playing in the surf and seagulls parrying over their catch engulfed us. Within moments Sadie put her head on my shoulder, stopped crying, and fell fast asleep. That weekend, my husband and I logged many hours of hiking along the seashore, with Sadie sleeping on our backs. And to this day there is nothing that soothes and relaxes her as easily as the sound of the surf.

The Book of Job is another biblical text in which God comforts and consoles us through nature. The message, which most of us are not familiar with despite the renown of the story, is similar to that of Psalm 23: "Get outside! See the sea and the sky, the eagles and the ostrich. Let Me be present with you through the majesty of Creation."

Job is a more lengthy text than Psalm 23, so I will just recap the pertinent parts. I should explain that the Book of Job is written in gorgeous, poetic verse, although, admittedly, it can be difficult to read. For the sake of comprehension, I will convert it to far less beautiful but much easier to understand language. When I use an actual quote, I will put it in italics and give the chapter and verse.

To begin with, you should know that the Book of Job

is perhaps the ultimate story of misfortune. Job was a pious man and extremely wealthy. Here is how he is described in the Bible:

> *There was a man in the land of Uz named Job. That man was blameless and upright; he feared God and shunned evil. Seven sons and three daughters were born to him; his possessions were seven thousand sheep, three thousand camels, five hundred yoke of oxen and five hundred she-asses, and a very large household. That man was wealthier than anyone in the East.* (Job 1:1–3)

The story continues, explaining that in just one day, and for no apparent reason, Job loses everything. His livestock are either stolen or mysteriously drop dead. The roof of his house collapses, killing all his children. And, finally, Job himself is stricken with a dreadful disease that covers every inch of his skin with painful, itchy sores. Yuck.

Job cries out to God for explanation, but his friends urge him to look at his own behavior instead. They insist, "You must have done something to deserve such misfortune!" But Job is adamant that he is without blame and does not deserve such torment. He continues to demand an explanation from God, and, eventually, God answers him. (Getting a direct answer from God is about the only enviable thing that happens to Job!)

Ironically, God actually had a very good explanation

for the lost livestock, dead children, and Job's itchy, boil-like things. In the first chapter of Job, God bragged to Satan about what a faithful servant Job was. Satan says, "Of course he is faithful, God! You give him everything. What does he have to complain about? He's got it all: kids, wealth, and good health. Take that away and I'll bet he will stop being so faithful." God accepts the wager and lets Satan take it all away!

So you see, God could have simply said, "Well, you know, Job, I'm sorry about your loss, but you see, I had this bet with Satan that if you lost your wealth, your kids, and your health, you would remain faithful to me. Satan thought you would stop being faithful to me, but I knew better. Thanks to you, I won the bet. Strong work, Job!"

At this point, of course, God could have taken a few cues from the Ministry of Magic from the Harry Potter series and used a memory-erasing charm, then given Job back his livestock, his children, and his fit and firm figure. No one would have been the wiser. After all, God had made the point to Satan.

But that's not what God does. God doesn't give Job books to read on grief, or tell him to pray. Nor does God say, "We are starting a support group for people who have lost their livestock, and their children, and have itchy, boil-like things all over their bodies. We meet Tuesdays at milking time, since no one has cows left to milk."

God does comfort Job, but not with an explanation. Rather God takes Job on a tour of Creation, from God's point of view. Nature—not text and not prayer—is what God uses to comfort his faithful servant. Can you imagine touring the expanses of the earth with the Creator of the Universe as your guide? God shows Job the ocean and says, "Feel the salty spray of the sea on your face? I set the boundary for the waves of the sea. I commanded them, *You may come so far and no farther; / Here your surging waves will stop"* (Job 38:11).

And then God points upward to the vast evening sky and says, "Look up above. See the shimmering stars in the sky? I placed each one carefully. That is the constellation Delphinus, the dolphin, playfully diving through the night sky. And there is Orion, the noble hunter, forever pursuing Taurus, the proud bull."

God shows Job soaring eagles and wild beasts, the ostrich with elegant plumes and feathers, the wild ass roaming across the salt lands. God shows Job the wild animals of the earth, rather than animals like dogs and cows that humans have tamed to do their bidding.

God also shows Job the far edges of the earth, the wilderness where God makes it rain even though no man roams. Humans are glaringly absent from this view of the world—a powerful reminder that Job, and humanity in general, is not the center of the universe!

In *The Book of Job,* the translator, Stephen Mitchell, describes the wilderness in gorgeous, poetic language designed to touch our hearts and souls, not just our intellect.

> *Who cuts a path for the thunderstorm*
> > *and carves a road for the rain—*
> *to water the desolate wasteland,*
> > *the land where no man lives;*
> *to make the wilderness blossom*
> > *and cover the desert with grass?*

After this whirlwind tour, how could one even attempt to reply? Job does venture a response, though, and his words are the crux of the story. Most Bibles erroneously translate Job's response as "Therefore, I abhor myself and repent in dust and ashes." But one must read the original Hebrew to see that the verse is more accurately translated as "Therefore I recant [my question], and am comforted that I am dust."*

Ultimately, Job is comforted. He is comforted by his whirlwind tour of the expanses of the natural world, through which he comes to recognize that he is connected to, but not the center of, the universe. He is comforted that he is part of

---

*For more information, see Stephen Mitchell, *The Book of Job* (New York: HarperPerennial, 1987).

this vast and intricate community and that he, like every other part of creation, comes from dust and returns to dust.

The fact that God never answers Job's question "Why did this happen to me?" even though there is an explanation, is beside the point. Nor will we ever in our grief get a satisfactory answer to "Why?" For example, why couldn't the young kayaker live a few more years? And why didn't Moses get to go into the Promised Land? We all wish Rabbi Harold Kushner had written a book called _Why_ Bad Things Happen to Good People rather than _When_ Bad Things Happen to Good People, but no one knows the answer to "why?" The story of Job, like Kushner's book, is about finding comfort even when one cannot find answers.

So there you have it. Two biblical passages, Psalm 23 and the Book of Job, both with similar messages: Go out into nature! Let the waters, trees, and grasses, the expanses, valleys, and heights, comfort you. Let them remind you that you are not alone but are part of something much larger than yourself. Let this be your comfort.

While organized, indoor religion doesn't generally recommend going outside and sitting by rivers and lakes during times of spiritual need, knowledge of the healing and cleansing powers of nature, and of water specifically, has survived through the generations in the rituals of mikvah (ritual bath) and its Christian offspring, baptism.

What is a mikvah? A mikvah is a special bath created

for ritual immersion. Its purpose is not physical cleansing (one bathes before entering) but spiritual purification.

Its traditional uses include immersion before conversion and marriage, on Sabbath and holidays (for men), and at the end of the menstrual cycle (for married women). Today, though, the mikvah is used for spiritual cleansing at many times of transition by those in "progressive" circles—transitions that include divorce, special birthdays, and graduating from college. During such transitions the connection that the Psalmist and Job found in nature would be reassuring.

So what makes a mikvah a natural experience? What links it to the still waters of the Psalmist and the salty breakers of Job's whirlwind tour? The water that fills a mikvah must be *mayim chayim* or "living waters." The water cannot pass through the pipes of the city water supply but must be collected directly from rain, springs, rivers, lakes, or oceans. How immeasurably different that water feels! It is fresh from the source, as if linking us all the way back to the waters of the Creation story and the rain that fell on Noah's flood, sent by God to cleanse the world.

For some, entering the mikvah is an intensely spiritual act. For all mikvah users, however, a visit to the mikvah can be leisurely and relaxing, a time out from the harried lifestyles we lead, a chance to be alone, to contemplate and reflect.

Before you enter the ritual bath there are several steps

of preparation. For example, first you soak in a steaming hot bath and scrub yourself from head to toe. You clip your nails and remove nail polish, so nothing comes between you and the cleansing water. Then, when you are ready, you enter the mikvah chamber itself. For me, stepping into the soft, warm water of the mikvah is like stepping into a realm where time stands still. As the water envelops me, I feel the embrace of my mother, my grandmother, my great-grandmother, a line of women stretching all the way back to the beginning of time. Through the living waters (which could be the same water they bathed in!) these women tenderly reach out across the centuries, gently washing away all my hurts and pains. As I feel the water flow across my arms and face I am reminded that whatever consumes me, it will pass, as everything does. Like the constant cycles of water—from cloud, to rain, to stream, to river, to ocean, and evaporating back again to clouds— I realize that in my life there are also cycles. Pain and despair, loneliness and remorse, do, in time, give way to joy and peace.

It is unfortunate that today the mikvah is often an uncomfortable experience that has little similarity to the natural experiences of the Psalmist and Job, or even to what a mikvah was like a century ago.

My great-grandmother Bubbe Tetzie said that in the old country the women used to go down to the river for their mikvah. It was a private place, where the river was covered with trees arching out across the waters. There she and her mother, and her mother before her, would step out of their clothes, leaving them folded on the bank, and immerse themselves in the bracing cold water of the river.

Today access to the mikvah is often limited because of halachic (Jewish law) considerations, and even if you are allowed in, it can be a disappointment. The mikvah is usually in a cramped, mildly musty basement, because Jewish law requires it to be in the ground so the water does not have to be conveyed through pipes. But even if the water is natural, there is little "natural" about the experience. Even a fancy basement (and there are some very beautiful mikvahs in very beautiful basements) is still a basement, with no windows, no views of mountains or trees, no bird songs or soft breezes. And everything about the mikvah experience is now ritualized, from the way in which you wash and immerse to the words of blessing you recite, so there is not much that is "natural" about it anymore.

But despite all that, the ancient roots of the mikvah present a wonderful opportunity to create a mikvah alternative that will help us to reclaim our ancient wisdom. We can create, and need to create, our own meaning-filled mikvah experiences. Here are some ideas for how to create your own mikvah.

Perhaps it will be finding a secluded swimming hole along the creek. Or it doesn't have to be immersion in water. It can also be any experience that allows you to immerse yourself in nature. Your backyard or city park may do just fine. Try a walk in the woods, where you can hear the sound of the chickadees and the cardinals. Or sit by a pond, your back against a strong willow tree trunk, and watch the Canadian geese paddle across the surface. My suggestions for creating alternative mikvahs are simple:

1. Go solo. This is a time to focus on your relationship to nature and through that portal to God, not to other people.
2. Set aside enough time so you can feel leisurely, but not so much that you feel obligated.
3. Find a place in nature that resonates for you.
4. Keep your intention and focus. Try not to sidestep into distracting thoughts.
5. Breathe deeply and let the sounds, smells, and sights of the natural world bathe you and hold you.
6. Remember, you are a member of this earthly community. Life is not "all about you," but neither are you ever completely alone.

Returning to the ancient wisdom of Psalm 23 and the Book of Job simply means getting out there and immersing yourself in nature. Let the wonder and beauty of the earth comfort, console, and inspire you. This wisdom is your heritage. Restore your soul beside still waters.

Throughout these chapters, we have explored this ancient biblical wisdom: "Let the wilderness awaken your spirituality." We have rediscovered a myriad of lessons that were lost when religion moved indoors. Remember, when our biblical ancestors wanted to reach God they did not go to church or synagogue. Rather they climbed mountains, sought out streams, or sat beneath majestic palms. Along with all the sacred texts they passed on to us, this relationship with the outdoors is also our birthright. We must reclaim it.

Today in our frenetic lives—where it seems impossible to get off the grid—wilderness, and nature in general, overflows with opportunities to deepen our spirituality and enrich our relationships with self, community, and God.

May we have the wisdom to seek out these spiritual portals, to protect these sacred natural places, to learn from them and to love them.

# Guardians of the Earth:
# To Till and to Tend

*How many are the things You have made,*
   *O Lord;*
*You have made them all with wisdom;*
*the earth is full of Your creations . . .*
*May the glory of the Lord endure forever.*

           —Psalm 104:24, 31

I once lived in a small tent, on a gravel bar, on the outskirts of a rainy Alaskan fishing town called Cordova. The town was so small that there were two roads, a handful of stop signs, and no traffic lights.

The main road started at the docks, where fishermen hauled supplies back and forth between town and their boats. From there the road headed up Main Street, past the post office, grocery store, general store, and café, and then headed out of town, past my gravel bar and finally a mile or so out to the canneries, where I worked. There the road curved back into the sea, where incessant waves washed onto the gravel.

Each morning at 4:30 a.m., my alarm jarred me from a deep sleep. The rain, which had lulled me to sleep at night, usually still played a tapping rhythm on the tent fly in the morning. I unzipped my sleeping bag quickly, like tearing off a Band-Aid so it won't hurt, and scrambled out into the tent vestibule where I kept my grimy work clothing. I liked to pretend this separation kept my tent somewhat clean.

I pulled on long underwear, wool pants, a shirt, and a fleece jacket, rain gear, boots, and finally my homemade knit hat, and stepped out into another Alaskan morning. I walked half a mile along the coast to the salmon processing plant, where I worked eighteen hours a day gutting fish on the "slime line." The factory was loud, despite my double set of earplugs; cold, despite my wool layers and rain gear; and smelly—oh, did it stink! The work was repetitive and tiresome—but the money was good.

Toward the middle of August, when the rains began in earnest, our makeshift campground began to flood. My neighbors and I put our tents up on wooden pallets, first one high, and then two high. One morning I awoke to strange thrashing sounds. I looked outside and saw that the gravel bar had practically become a lake, and the salmon were trying to swim across it. But the water was so low that the salmon couldn't actually swim, so they just sort of thrashed up against the gravel, indignantly pushing their way through the rocks, and many were suffocating in the low water.

A local explained that the river used to flow fast and free through what was now our campground. But when the area had been mined for gravel, a few years ago, the river had been redirected a quarter mile to the east, and the salmon, which had spawned in that river for centuries, had not gotten the memo that the river had been moved. When it is time for salmon to lay eggs, they swim upriver, back home—and even if the river that used to be home is no longer there, they still try to "go home," so to speak.

When I lived in Alaska, it was easy to see firsthand the interconnectedness of human beings and nature. Every day I saw the impact of our choices on the land and sea around us, and I became acutely aware of the power and resilience of nature, but also of its vulnerability.

Now that I live in the lower forty-eight, however, it is much more difficult to get the connection between driving my SUV and the heat we've been sweating in all summer. Paying $60 to fill my gas tank, or cranking on the air-conditioning, hurts my wallet, but it's just not the same as having confused salmon swim through your living room.

Sometimes, being environmentally responsible—recycling and biking instead of driving, and so forth—feels as futile as the experience of trying to save money by just ordering a sandwich and iced tea for dinner, and ending up splitting the check with ten people who all ordered steak dinners and an expensive bottle of wine. What good can just one person do? Why should I bother installing high-efficiency lightbulbs when every driveway on the block has an SUV parked in it?

As always, I come back to my moral compass, religion. As Carl Pope, the executive director of the Sierra Club, said on a recent conference call with Jewish environmental leaders, "Morality doesn't help you stop hitting your own thumb with a hammer. But it does stop you from hurting people far away, or in the future." Our treatment of the planet is not just a scientific or political issue, it is a moral issue. So what does religion teach us is our role in regard to nature? And what does the Bible tell us is the right thing to do?

One of the first things God does in the Bible, directly after placing Adam in the Garden of Eden, is to lay out Adam's job description: "The Lord God took the man and placed him in the garden of Eden, to till it and tend it" (Genesis 2:15).

Although Judaism offers a lot of amazing thousand-year-old laws that still apply to the environment today, the crux of the Bible's ecological arguments is this verse itself: "to till it and tend it." The earth is not ours; we are simply caretakers of it. Our job is "to till and to tend" God's Creation, the earth.

Unfortunately, a lot of fuss has been made about a verse that comes a bit earlier in the Bible. In the first Creation story, God creates man in His image and then commands him, "Be fruitful, and multiply, and replenish the earth, and *subdue it:* and *have dominion over* the fish of the sea, and over the birds of the air, and over every living thing that moves upon the earth" (Genesis 1:28). (JB)

For years some religious people and corporations have argued that this passage gives us the right to fill the earth, subdue it, and have dominion over every living thing on the planet. Those who hold this view believe that within this verse, God gives us the earth, and all that it holds, as a toolbox of resources, to use as we see fit. The "subdue and have dominion" verse has been used as a mandate for everything from strip-mining, to clear-cutting, to habitat destruction.

But, unfortunately for those who use this verse to prove their point of view, just one chapter later we find a verse that counters the first one. The tricky thing about Bible study is that you can never read any verse in isolation, because each verse is explained by other verses throughout the Bible. The art of Bible study therefore involves hopping back and forth between texts to find the passages that explain each other, as in the "subdue and have dominion" verse, which is clarified by the "to till and to tend" verse.

I'm not saying that the "subdue and have dominion" verse is wrong. There is no denying that we have dominion over the earth. No other species in history has held the power to destroy life on the planet. In fact, we can choose from a variety of ways to destroy the earth, or at least change it so that life as we know it will no longer exist.

We can choose between quick death by pushing a few buttons that launch nuclear missiles, or slow death by poisoning our air and contaminating our water sources. And of course climate change provides another frightful option. Yes, we have subdued the earth and we do have dominion over it. The urgent question is, what is our dominion supposed to look like? This is what is unclear in the excerpt of biblical text.

Fortunately, Genesis 2:15 answers the question about dominion and clarifies any ambiguity. It tells us that we are supposed to be protectors; we are supposed "to till and tend" God's garden and take care of God's planet. There is also a breathtaking passage in the Jewish scriptural text Midrash Ecclesiastes Rabbah, written around 800 CE, which says, "When God created the first human beings, God led them around the garden of Eden and said: 'Look at my works! See how beautiful they are—how excellent! For your sake I created them all. See to it that you do not spoil and destroy My world; for if you do, there will be no one else to repair it."

I am amazed that these prescient words were written so many years ago, and that even then there was concern that we might spoil and destroy the earth. This additional text makes it clear that although God made the earth for us, God did not intend for us to use it recklessly. It is God's earth, not ours. "Take good care of it," God commands. What a clear call to action! Fortunately, today many religious leaders have come to understand this message and many churches and synagogues are now leaders in the environmental movement.

For me, an equally strong call to action, and perhaps an even stronger argument for taking care of the earth, comes from something more immediate than the text. Some of my colleagues wonder, What could be stronger than the words of the Bible? My answer: the feeling I have when I am outdoors, riding my bike past a green pasture filled with blue chicory flowers as far as my eye can see, or sitting on the red rock high above town and watching a hawk ride the thermals round and round.

In this book you have read about my outdoor journeys as well as the experiences of participants on Adventure Rabbi trips. You've read what a potent place nature is for many of us, a place of indescribable connection, ripe with spiritual awakenings. If you are like me and experience your most powerful spiritual moments outdoors, the mandate is clear. We must take care of the planet, for as we destroy the earth (either through action or lack thereof) we destroy our opportunity for spirit, and we destroy ourselves.

The Bible gives us a number of amazing laws to guide our treatment of the natural world. One of the most often cited is called Ba'al Tashhit: "You shall not destroy." It is based on the biblical passage Deuteronomy 20:19, which reads, "When in your war against a city you have to besiege it a long time in order to capture it, you must not destroy its trees, wielding the ax against them."

The original biblical law is simple: do not destroy fruit trees during war. However, ecological destruction was a common practice even in biblical warfare. For example, in Judges we read that Avimelech "razed the town and sowed it with salt" (Judges 9:45). And not much has changed; for example, consider the deforestation of the Vietnamese countryside during the Vietnam War.

But the law was gradually expanded through the centuries from a prohibition against cutting down fruit trees during war to a prohibition against waste in general. The first expansions of the law began two thousand years ago, when the rabbis concluded that if the Bible ordered us to protect the trees during war, we should avoid all ecological destruction during war. Then they realized that the law should apply to peacetime as well. After all, it is far easier to be ecologically aware during peacetime than when bombs are falling all around you. For the rabbis of old, the bottom line was this: the earth belongs to God, not us; it is our responsibility to take care of God's earth.

With this responsibility in mind, the rabbis eventually expanded the law to include any sort of wasteful activity involving natural or human-made things, during wartime or peacetime. Neither the exploitation of natural resources nor waste in general, said the rabbis, is acceptable.

Look at these ancient prohibitions and notice which ones still make sense today:

- You may not feed livestock polluted water.*
- You may not divert or destroy a river, if it affects the supply of man, animals, or plants.†
- You may not build anything producing foul odors, such as tanneries or cemeteries, inside the city or upwind of the city.‡
- You may not wantonly break vessels, tear garments, destroy buildings, or throw away food.§

Today we are called upon to apply these laws to promote a wide range of efforts to decrease waste. In this spirit, at a recent Sabbath service my congregants began

---

*Based on Babylonian Talmud Avoda Zarah 30b.
†Based on Babylonian Talmud Pesachim 5a, Midrash Sifre to Deuteronomy 203 and Rabbi Moses Maimonides, Mishneh Torah, Book of Judges, Laws of Kings and Wars 6:10.
‡Based on Babylonian Talmud Baba Batra 25a.
§Based on Rabbi Moses Maimonides, Mishneh Torah, Book of Judges, Laws of Kings and Wars 6:10.

brainstorming ways to obey the command "Do not waste!" My goal was to create a list of the "Ten Commandments of Conscious Consumption." My community, however, said, "You should list twenty so everyone can choose the ten that work for them." Imagine if the Bible's Ten Commandments were written by committee so we could pick and choose! Which ten would you leave out? Nonetheless, here are the twenty so you can pick the ones that work for you!

1. Don't buy things you don't need.
2. Support businesses and products that have sustainability policies.
3. Buy local products and produce, organic and free-range foods.
4. Install compact fluorescent lightbulbs (CFL) and turn off lights when not in use. (If we all replaced one conventional bulb with a CFL, it would lessen pollution as much as removing a million cars from the road.)
5. Buy high-efficiency appliances.
6. Use ecofriendly cleaning products.
7. Lower your heat and lessen your air-conditioning.
8. Telecommute whenever possible.
9. When it is time to replace your car, buy a fuel-efficient vehicle.

10. Use wind or solar power for your home and office.

11. Drive less: ride your bike and walk more.

12. Reduce, reuse, recycle (i.e., encourage the use of hand-me-down clothing, toys, sporting goods, and electronics).

13. Install dual-2 flush toilets (different flow amounts based on need).

14. Bring your own reusable cloth bags to the grocery store.

15. Compost.

16. Choose products that contain less packaging. (About one-third of the waste in our landfills is from packaging materials!)

17. Vacation near home so you can fly less.

18. Don't use wrapping paper or store-bought greeting cards.

19. Use less water.

20. Encourage our politicians to create policies that enable us to stop giving oil money to people who hate us and want to kill us.

On a recent Adventure Rabbi hike, one of the participants pointed out that the same habits that contribute to spiritual anemia—for example, not taking time to rest, pause, notice, and appreciate, as well as not taking respon-

sibility for our own lives—are the ones that lead to ex-
ploiting the planet. Let me explain.

We all know what happens when we don't have time
to stop and just chill. For example, we rush so fast that we
fail to notice the world around us (think of Moses and the
burning bush). Or we don't make time to really connect
with family and friends (think of the story about the doctor and his family). When our lives are too full, we starve
our souls by not making the spiritual connection that we so
desperately crave.

When some of us are spiritually unsatisfied we experience a subtle discontentedness, like a deep itch we just
can't scratch, so we just learn to deal with it. Others sink
into depression. Either way, our society has taught us to
deal with this in two ways:

1. Buy more stuff.
2. Buy more stuff.

Consume, consume, consume! Marketers have done
well. We all know that people with flat TVs are much hap-
pier than those of us with old-fashioned TV sets. And what
can bring as much joy as a new, even smaller cell phone
with a built-in video camera and MP3 player, or a new
mountain bike with full suspension, or a vacation to an exotic beach resort?

Studies have proven that our happy meters do go up

when we buy the [fill in the blank] we so desperately "needed." But unfortunately, the effect is only temporary. A subtle, lingering dissatisfaction with life abides, until we buy again.

The side effect of all this consumerism is, of course, waste. What do we do with all this stuff? What about all the energy it took to manufacture, pack, and ship it? When I lived in Alaska, I could fit everything I owned into the back of a Honda Civic hatchback. Now? Not so much. All my religious books wouldn't even fit in a Civic. My various versions of the Bible alone would fill up the entire backseat, and my trail guides and natural history books would take up the rest of the space! I'm not saying we should sell off our worldly possessions and live out of the back of our cars, especially not small hatchbacks. But I am suggesting that if you are like me, it wouldn't hurt to be a little more aware of what we buy, why we buy it, and what we do with the things the new stuff replaces. Shopping has become an activity unto itself, and how often do we shop out of boredom rather than to supply a real need?

Ironically, the more we shop and consume, the less likely we are to notice the raw beauty that surrounds us. Instead of seeking the serenity of green pastures and still waters, where true spiritual fulfillment awaits us, we go to Target, Home Depot, and Best Buy, where bargains on things we don't really need eagerly await us.

When we disconnect ourselves from natural places,

we fail to see firsthand the impact our lives are having on the earth. Not surprisingly, often the people who are most passionate about protecting the environment are those who have taken the time to be in wild spaces, to climb the peaks and paddle the creeks. Ah, the peace of wild places!

Last Sabbath my husband and I climbed Notch Mountain, a 13,237-foot peak. We took a back route that is seldom traveled, and the trail, overgrown by grass and moss, was delightfully difficult to find. It was like hiking used to be twenty-five years ago—although not exactly. The big difference was the air quality. For miles around, a haze covered the mountains and valleys. Why? Because the warmer days and longer summer seasons have created a population boom of bark beetles, which infest the pine trees. The nights are no longer cold enough, or the early autumn frosts frequent enough, to kill them off. Nothing kills them, so the bark beetles kill the trees with abandon. Then the dead trees fall to the forest floor, creating fuel for the ferocious forest fires sweeping these parts of the country. The haze in the air is the lingering smoke. Ah wilderness, how vulnerable it is and how quickly it is disappearing.

I realize how fortunate I am to be able to walk up to the top of my street and be in a wild place, home to mountain lions and bears. Boulder, Colorado, is surrounded by open space and our city council is a national leader on environmental policy. The city started buying up the surrounding lands and preserving them as open space in the

1890s. Where did they get such a radical idea? Is it possible that they read it in the Bible? The Bible commands us to leave open spaces around our cities: "You shall also give to the Levites an open space for the cities. And they shall have the cities to live in; and their open space shall be for their animals, their substance, and all their needs of life" (Numbers 35:2–3) (author's translation).* And building on this, the Talmud, the major book of Jewish law, says that "It is forbidden to live in a city that does not have greenery" (based on Jerusalem Talmud Kiddushin 4:12).

But what does the Bible mean that open space shall be for "all their needs of life"? One of the greatest biblical scholars of all time, Rashi, taught that this meant that the open space was not for animals, farming, or houses but simply to beautify the city. Think of Central Park in New York City, which some say is the heart and soul of Manhattan. Can you even image how much poorer New York City would be, spiritually, without that park? Or your town without a park or greenery? Another of our great rabbis, Maimonides, taught that every city must have 1,500 feet of open space.† His son, Rav Abraham ben Moses Maimonides, explained the importance of open space: "The

---

*Author's translation of the original Hebrew as based on Rashi commentary on Numbers 35:2–3, *Chumash with Rashi commentary,* edited by Rabbi A. M. Silbermann (Jerusalem: Feldhein Publishers, 1934), p. 166.

†*The Code of Maimonides: Book Seven, The Book of Agriculture* (New Haven, CT: Yale University Press, 1979), pp. 400–401.

enjoyment of the beauties of nature, such as the contemplation of flower-clad meadows, lofty mountains and majestically flowing rivers, is essential to the spiritual development of even the holiest people."*

Ironically, sometimes it is not the lack of open space that keeps us away from nature, it is lack of time. This is part of the reason that Sabbath, our supposedly nonoptional day off, is so important environmentally. Sabbath is one of the most powerful, ecological balancing mechanisms in the Bible, because "Sabbath rest" gives us time to go enjoy being in nature. As we discussed in the chapter about Sabbath, six days a week we are supposed to be out in the world, striving to make it a better place. We do amazing things—we discover vaccines to cure illness, we create insecticides to stop blight from killing our crops, we negotiate treaties that stop people from killing one another. But on the seventh day, we are told to refrain from both creating and destroying. Rather we should sit back and notice that the world exists. We should take time to see the burning bushes and to give ourselves a chance to experience the awesomeness of God's Creation. This also gives us time to notice the side effects of all our accomplishments. The Sabbath doesn't negate the importance of our weekday work; it just gives us a bit of perspective. Ulti-

*Rabbi Abraham ben Maimonides, as quoted in Rabbi David E. Stein, *A Garden of Choice Fruit* (Washington, DC: Shomrei Adamah, 1991), p. 68.

mately, the day of rest should remind us that the earth is God's Creation, not ours, but we are the gardeners, and we are morally obligated to care for God's Creation, "to till and to tend" God's garden.

So how have we been doing at fulfilling our job description? Not so well, I'm afraid. And now the real question facing us, the new conversation in which we must engage, is what are we going to do about it? Our religion—the Bible—tells us without ambiguity what we must do, and our hearts, inspired by the tall trees and vibrant flowers, also tell us what we must do. We must be guardians of the earth. We each must take personal responsibility for our impact on the planet. We must be Nachshon and take the first step, and then others will join us.

May we have the wisdom, the tenacity, and the fortitude to help God's garden endure. In the words of the Psalmist:

> *How many are the things You have made, O Lord;*
> *You have made them all with wisdom;*
> *the earth is full of Your creations . . .*
> *May the glory of the Lord endure forever.*
>
> (Psalm 104:24, 31)

# Resources for
# Continuing the Adventure

Frequently, people who come on Adventure Rabbi trips say, "Wow, I didn't know there were so many people like me in the world!" My first suggestion, if you want to continue to learn with me and other like-minded people, is to join an Adventure Rabbi trip or High Holiday retreat, or bring me to your community. But even if you can't come on an Adventure Rabbi program, we can help you meet like-minded people on the Web and in your part of the world.

Visit the Web site www.AdventureRabbi.org to follow up on these ideas:

- **Join our social networking community.** Meet like-minded people who like to do what you like to do.
- **Host a book discussion group.** Download free materials to host your own book discussion group. We'll give you all the tools you need to

start a new group (we may even be able to help you find members) or help you strengthen an existing book club.

- **Plan or join an Adventure Rabbi–style hike in your area.** Download program materials to plan a hike in your area, based on one of the book chapters.

- **Share your thoughts.** Our moderated discussion board gives readers an opportunity to discuss religion, nature, and spirituality with other like-minded readers and encourages people to get together in their regional areas to discuss the book, as well as enjoy nature together.

- **Form an Adventure Rabbi environmental action group.** Our online material and e-mail action updates will help you to form a local action group and help you to initiate environmental actions in your area.

- **Learn more and meet the Adventure Rabbi.** Our online calendar features upcoming book discussion groups, book signings by the author, ecological initiatives, and book tour information.